SIGNALMAN'S NIGHTMARE

SIGNALMAN'S NIGHTMARE

ADRIAN VAUGHAN

GUILD PUBLISHING LONDON

© Adrian Vaughan 1987

This edition published 1987
by Book Club Associates
by arrangement with
John Murray (Publishers) Ltd

Typeset by Inforum Ltd, Portsmouth
Printed and bound in Great Britain
at The Bath Press, Avon

For the women in my life:

Susan

Rebecca, Constance and Beatrice

*Say not thou, What is the cause that the former
    days were better than these?
For thou dost not inquire wisely concerning
    this.*

Ecclesiastes 7:10

CONTENTS

ACKNOWLEDGEMENTS

It is recorded that on 24 February 1869 a boy went for a footplate ride over the West London line of the GWR. For taking the lad, Driver Henry Barney was fined 5 shillings. So locomotive trespass goes back to 1869 and even as far back, I suggest, as the opening of the Liverpool & Manchester Railway. Unauthorised visitors in signal boxes arrived with the first signal box. Trespassing by interested persons, from small boys to bishops, was frequent and part of the railway. Punishments for the offending railwaymen appear to have been rare — otherwise the practice would have ceased. The Reverend A.H. Malan rode the footplates of broad-gauge expresses in the 1880s; my friend Bill Kenning (referred to in this volume) gave me photographic proof of his locomotive and signal box trespassing before the First World War; another friend, P.S.A. Berridge — who later became Chief Civil Engineer (Bridges) for the GWR and BRWR — was a locomotive trespasser during and after the First World War; and I can testify to my own misdemeanours in this field shortly after the Second World War. I was passionately interested in the railway, and, in the humanitarian spirit inherited from earlier generations of drivers and signalmen, I was invited onto engines and into signal boxes. I do not know the names of any of these kind men except for Signalman Harold Summerfield, so first I should like to thank him and all the other railwaymen of forty years ago who encouraged me to become, eventually, a railwayman — something of which I am very proud. I would like to thank many workmates for spending hours talking to me about their careers and telling me the legend of that particular piece of line described in these pages; all of them were the kindest of men: Signalmen Tom Baber, Mick Elliot, Sid Fleming, Patrolman

Dick Kerslake, Driver Don Kingdom, Signalman Ron Kirby, Sid Mumford, Ron Reynolds, Jack Richards, Ken Russell, Signal and Telegraph Lineman John Taylor, Driver Charlie Turner, Signalmen Fred Wilkins and Stan Worsfold. My thanks are also due to friends and relatives who helped me to produce this book: Chris Burden, David Collins, Ian Coulson, David Hyde, Graham and Betty Mitchell and my sister Frances and her husband Camilus for their hospitality during my researching sessions in London, John Morris, Bill Noke and Keith Philbrick. Duncan McAra and Jeannie Brooke Barnet of John Murray deserve my thanks for their encouragement in what has been quite a difficult task. Last, but by no means least, I must thank my wife Susan and my daughters Rebecca, Constance and Beatrice for putting up with me when I got bad tempered while the book was being difficult.

ILLUSTRATIONS

The photographs were taken by the author, with the exception of 1 (Dr Jack Hollick/author's collection); 2 (Peter Barlow/author's collection); 4 (W.L. Kenning); and 11, 12 (H.O. Vaughan)

DIAGRAMS

PROLOGUE

I do not remember a time when I was not passionately interested in railways. The embankment of the Southern Railway formed the eastern boundary of Palmer Park in Reading, my home town, and on the embankment was the distant signal for Kennet Spur signal box: a yellow arm on a grimy, lattice-work mast which was known to me in my pre-school years as the 'Yellow Signal' on account of the colour of the arm. I knew nothing, in 1945, of the purpose of a distant signal to act as a 'Caution' for a 'Stop' signal ahead. I knew only that when an arm was horizontal it meant 'stop' and when raised it meant 'go' and when that particular signal was raised it heralded the swift passage of a steam or electric train running smartly down the hill from Earley. So when I first saw a train go past the arm, when it was in its horizontal position, I was alarmed — like any good railwayman at this apparent disregard for safety — and ran home to tell my mother and frantically demand that she do something about it.

Railways were the greatest free show available to boys of all ages anywhere in Britain. I grew up with them by day, and at night I often lay awake and listened to the clashing ring of shunted wagon buffers or the rhythmic snorting of a labouring goods engine in the toils of Earley bank, five minutes out of the yard and already short of steam. On the Southern Railway during 1945–9 there were at work the tall-chimneyed, gang-ling, erstwhile express engines of the London & South West-ern Railway, the South Eastern & Chatham and even of the long-defunct London, Chatham & Dover Railway. They hauled grass-green carriages, knobbly-looking vehicles with much moulding around their small windows, panelled sides, a raised, glazed roof section at one end and a double row of ventilators on their roofs like so many steel sea-shells.

When I started school, in January 1946, I discovered the Great Western and its elegance and quite looked down upon the puny Southern with its vintage trains, not realising that for the Southern, Reading was the terminus of a branch line, while for the Great Western, Reading was a very important junction on their most important main line. With the exception of one unforgivably bad-tempered porter on Reading West station and one strict foreman on Reading (GWR) engine shed whose sense of responsibility did not allow him to let little boys to trespass, the railwaymen I met in my schooldays were invariably friendly. So I trespassed warily on the strict foreman's domain but trespassed wantonly on locomotive footplates and in the little signal box called Woodley Bridge in Sonning Cutting.

By the age of eleven, when our family moved out to Childrey, in the Vale of the White Horse, I fancied I had a fair notion of how to operate a small signal box and, in theory at any rate, I knew how to drive a steam engine. I also thought I knew about railwaymen. They seemed to be the most humane and understanding of men who were prepared to break the rules so that I could share in the fascination of their somewhat secret world. Each footplate was a Kingdom and the driver was King – although he would have been useless without his good fireman mate. Each signal box was as remote as a lighthouse yet inside each box there was a busy life, a constant communication with other boxes, carrying out an essential job under the hands of the best of men.

The station for Childrey was Challow and there I found the usual, friendly welcome in a relatively large and certainly very busy signal box. Twice a day, three times a week, I could ride around the station on the engine of the Fly, the local, pick-up goods. At Challow on the Fly I was able to put my driving theory into practice, first with the driver's large hand over mine, then, when we had both gained confidence, on my own. Railwaymen felt sure that this freedom was part of the natural order of life otherwise they would not have allowed me the privileges they so freely gave. I felt free to learn and to enjoy the beauties of machinery and the intricacies of railway life.

When I joined the railway at Challow in September 1960 after nearly five years in the army, I joined with men, who were already friends, to give an enthusiastic service to the local community. I constructed a garden — which the GWR had omitted to provide when they rebuilt the station in the 1930s — and cosseted the passengers so that they felt welcome and comfortable. In doing this I did no more than was being done at a thousand country stations; there was an entirely selfish feeling of satisfaction to be gained from 'soft-soaping' the passengers just to see the appreciation on their faces. There was also a great deal of pleasure to be gained in the company of the old-hand railwaymen and in the stories they told as we worked on jobs that had changed little or not at all since railways began: loading, sheeting and roping down wagon-loads of produce or manufactures, writing out wagon labels and waybills in the dusty office of the great, brick, goods shed which was undoubtedly part of Brunel's original Great Western Railway and which Western Region, sadly, later pulled down.

From the Dickensian desk and stool of the goods shed, the shunting pole and the fresh flowers in the waiting room at Challow I went to the late Victorian signal box at Uffington, built in the year of Queen Victoria's Diamond Jubilee. There were certainly better signalmen than I; I probably did not have the best temperament for the job but there was none more enthusiastic for the job. I rode the footplates of many engines, often acting as fireman, sometimes even as driver — all strictly against the rules, of course. I visited many signal boxes. I learnt about the skills of the manually operated railway, the folklore and the morale that enables men to carry out hard, dirty work (in the case of steam engines) with cheerfulness and even enthusiasm. The underpinning of the steam-hauled railway was the sense of loyalty to the past, the sense of present challenge to which one rose and conquered and, finally, the sense of continuity which gave us all a feeling of security for the future. Albert Stanley, who had taught me my duties at Challow in 1960, had begun his service in 1920 at Dauntsey where he had learnt his first lessons from a man who had begun his service on the broad (7 ft) gauge Great Western in 1870. So long as we had steam engines and semaphore signalling the railway was essentially Victorian but, unfortunately, in the mid-1960s neither Management nor Government thought of this as a virtue. The strength or charm of working on the railway then was to be on this rare penisula of time, a land of old-fashioned manual work and reliability, jutting out into an ever-rising ocean of 'efficiency', unreliability and built-in redundancy.

I became a signalman at Challow shortly before the flood-tide of 'modernity' swamped and swept away first the station and its service to the community, then whole main lines and, finally, a way of life. As one among many railwaymen who was drowned I can hardly be expected to be grateful to the waves.

Adrian Vaughan
January 1987

CHAPTER ONE

BLISSFUL IGNORANCE

I started my first week as signalman at Challow on night shift during March 1962, driving down to the station in a Morris 8 saloon whose 1935 vintage headlamps sent out six-volt light through kitchen glass 'lenses'. The car was parked in Brunel's cavernous goods shed opposite the signal box, bright as a lighthouse in the night. I stopped at the side of the up relief line to see if it was safe to cross the four tracks and was in time to see and hear Jim Spinage belling the 9.50 p.m. Swindon to York express, the 'tinging' of the bells and the muffled 'whump, thump' of the levers being swung over by Jim's stout arms and strong back. The interior of the box looked splendid at five minutes to ten at night when the red, blue, black and yellow levers with their long, brass badges and burnished steel handles flashed like a full-dress military parade under the stark light of three electric bulbs. The glass-like linoleum floor covering reflected the colours, the fire was bright and so was Jim's 'going home' smile. He was soon away on his BSA Bantam motor-cycle leaving me in sole charge of four main lines and fifty-one levers until six o'clock next morning. I felt like a one-time pupil of a school, returned as a master.

I took my job at Challow more seriously than I had done at Uffington, because Uffington was only a 'passing' box while Challow had the important function of 'regulating' trains — each up or down train's progress had to be carefully monitored to see if there was a case for diverting it to the relief line to allow a following, faster train to overtake. We called this 'margining'. I was most concerned that there should be no delay to a passenger train because of my bad margining; I had to be more alert to the developing traffic situation; I had more duties in disseminating train-running information up and down the line; and, as the nights wore on, I became far more tired at Challow than I had been at Uffington. Later I would become fitter, more used to the strain. On the Saturday morning of my first week at Challow, the 2.45 a.m. Swindon 'Loco Yard' to Bordesley goods had clanked sedately past up the main line at 4 a.m. This was followed by a 'light' engine for Oxford which was standing at my up home signal as the 'Loco Yard' cleared the Intermediate Block Section signals at Circourt, about 1½ miles eastwards. Had I not been so tired I would have realised that the goods was travelling rather slower than usual and that, as the Milford Haven to Paddington sleeping car train would be following the 'light' engine, that engine ought to go 'up the shute' (up relief line) to Wantage Road, out of the way of the Milford. What I did was to allow the engine to come up the main line towards the signal box and no sooner had I done this than I realised my mistake. I went to the window with a red light to stop the engine and give its driver instructions that would rectify the error. The engine was a 'Grange'.

'Go up past Number Three and stop clear of the points. When you get the dummy* go back into the platform loop,' I shouted to the driver.

He gave me a disgusted look and set off. I gave 'Train out of Section' — 2–1 on the bell — to Elwyn Richards at Uffington and gave him 'Line Clear' when he rang out four beats for the Milford. I set the points for the engine but signal 42 simply would not budge; it had probably not been used for years. I felt frustration in that I could not make this rare movement and I felt panic that, with the 'Loco Yard' somewhere between me and Wantage and this engine also occupying the up main line, the Milford sleeper was going to be delayed as a result of my error. The next feeling was a desperate resolve that I would not be beaten and that I could still retrieve the situation. I replaced the points and, with a white light waved from side to side out of the signal box window, I called the driver back to the box. I

---

* The ground signal.

told him to go back outside the home signal and enter the relief line when I lowered the signal. Without a word but with a look that said it all, he went on his way.

That I had violated the most sacred regulation in the book hardly occurred to me then. In my tired and inexperienced state all that mattered to me was that the Milford should not be delayed on my account. As I turned the relief-line points for the engine standing outside the up home signal Elwyn sent the 'Train entering Section' signal — two beats on the bell — the Milford was passing Uffington, three minutes away. The sound of that high-pitched bell was like a sharp knife through my head as suddenly I realised the position in which I had placed many innocent people as well as myself. The men on the 'Grange' took ages to blow off their brake. I stood at the open window listening to the hoarse 'haaa' of the ejector and knew that the driver was deliberately 'hanging the pot on' to show his annoyance with me. The sound of the sleeping car train, drumming along at about 55 mph, came creeping through the night air; several seconds passed agonisingly before the 'Grange' made its first 'chuff' and began to move — very slowly — inside the protection of the home signal which I slammed back to 'Danger' because several lives and my job depended on it. As soon as the track circuit cleared and unlocked the points I heaved the levers over, setting the route for the main line before snatching 'off' the up main signals: 2,3,5 and 1 in that order. I heard an answering 'toot' from the unsuspecting driver of the Milford who, seeing my distant signal change from amber 'Caution' to green 'All Clear' right in front of his cab, thought merely that I had been late in 'pulling off' as a result of sleepiness.

As the Milford sailed by, the 'Loco Yard' cleared Wantage Road. I 'got the road' for the Milford on the main line and for the engine on the relief line and pulled over the necessary levers. The telephone at the far end of the up platform rang in the box and I answered it. 'That fast was following us pretty tight, wasn't it?' It was the driver of the 'Grange' who must have seen my frantic flurry of activity. His voice was quiet, sarcastic yet also a little menacing. 'We all depend on you people, you know.' Before I could make any reply — and apart from apologies there was nothing to say — he mercifully replaced the telephone and drove away.

I did not allow my early stupidity to overshadow my enjoyment of the job but used the event to become a better signalman. I loved the box when the rain was streaming down the windows and the wind was howling through the telephone wires outside on their tall poles. The interior of the box then was so clean and warm and everything was proceeding in such an orderly way. I walked easily from bells and instruments to levers to train register whilst all outside seemed to be at the mercy of the storm. I loved the box, too, on those early summer or early autumn mornings when the sun was low and bright, making the dawn mist the colour of champagne and the locomotive's exhaust a dazzling white over a black smokebox and red buffer beam. I liked the job in the summer heat when all the windows were open; Sam or Albert — one of the porters from the station — would be reclining in my armchair with a mug of tea, while I leant on the bar at the window to watch a train go by, checking it for all the things a signalman looked for to ensure safety. I watched the engine and its crew, checked all wheels for sparks from dragging brakes or flames from over-heated axleboxes, listened for untoward noises, looked for insecure doors, watched to see if the guard was trying to give me a message. Above all, I loved the box when it was really busy, when many arrangements had to be made and trains switched from line to line — such as at Christmas with all the 'Parcel Post' extra trains that ran among the usual traffic and the additional, Christmas excursions.

Those people who wanted to visit the signal box had to be decent types, people who were genuinely interested — or at least had the sense not to distract me. Two of my 'regulars' at Challow were Gladys and her niece Pauline whom I met while they were searching the lineside for wild flowers. They were caught in a sudden, summer thunderstorm and were already well soaked when they came hurrying past the box, going back to their car. I invited them in and that was the start of a very pleasant friendship which is still recalled and which resulted in the marriage of one of the ladies to a Challow signalman. On Sunday afternoons, when the box had been polished and there was a long gap in the train service, I would take a walk around the estate to see if everything was in order. One afternoon I set out to walk to my down advanced starting signal, 783 yards. At the far end of the stroll I slipped off the sleeper-end and wrenched my ankle painfully, so much so that I had to hop and hobble the whole distance back to the box. On the up-side horse-dock a family of four watched this procedure in silent amazement. At the box door I leant on the wall and called across to the father to ask if he felt like spending an hour or two pulling levers under my direction as I would be quite unable to do the job.He leaped at the opportunity and, under my instructions, did what was necessary with the levers whilst I hopped about to see to the bells, phones and train register. He, too, became a regular visitor to the box.

My most frequent caller, apart from station staff, was Bill Kenning. I had first met Bill in April 1964 at Haddenham where I had gone to photograph 4079 *Pendennis Castle* hauling an excursion to the Festiniog Railway. I was using one of my father's large, old plate cameras on a tripod. The camera — a Marion 'Tropical Soho' quarter-plate — had a body of polished teak, honey coloured, admirably embellished with brass fittings and red leather bellows. Bill, a connoisseur of anything out of the ordinary, spotted it from his perch in the signal box 300 yards away and came hurrying down the line for a closer look. He was a most out-of-the-ordinary person, completely mad about trains. We were friends at once. A few days later he sent me notice of his impending arrival at Challow in the form of a pseudo railway 'extra train notice': 'SPECIAL: DITCHLING TO CHALLOW, 'A' HEADCODE. THIS TRAIN MUST RUN PUNCTUALLY.' This was followed by a time-table of the journey, including stops for 'water' at various hostelries. When he got to the signal box he handed me his 'guard's log' wherein it appeared that he had arrived several minutes ahead of the time which was, in his own words, 'simply priceless'. He was about sixty-five, of medium height and build, with a clipped, white, military moustache, an accent straight out of the glove compartment of a Rolls-Royce and that curiously languid elegance of an upper-crust Englishman who is absolutely sure of himself and his place in the world. However, the one thing Bill was not was a snob — he was too much of a gentleman for that.

He had driven up from deepest Sussex in his Riley 'Redwing', an open car looking like a bath tub on solid steel, disc wheels. He had bought it new in 1923 when he was an undergraduate at Merton College, Oxford; it had survived the destruction of several gear boxes on impromptu 'hill-climbing trials' up Headington hill; he had driven his bride, Kathleen, away from the church in it and he had been driving it ever since. He drove into the station yard honking its klaxon and waving a guard's green flag, his tweed cap firmly and squarely down on his head. Looking down from the signal box I could see that the car was painted GWR green (he told me later that the paint came from Swindon factory) and was lined out in black and orange panels; touches of brass here and there set the colour scheme off nicely. There was a lot of rubbish piled on the back seat and, staring hard, I began to see that he had a large pile of rooks' nests, a bicycle and a bundle of chimney-sweeping rods. Had I been able to see inside I would have noticed some ceramic insulators off telephone-pole cross-bars, some oily cotton waste and the top lid of an engine driver's tea can. On the back bumper was a large red disc bearing the white letters LV — Last Vehicle — a relic of the London, Brighton & South Coast Railway which used such devices by day instead of tail lamps.

Bill was the only visitor I had who signed himself into and out of the box in the train register. The first time he did this I was alarmed; 'The Book' was not the place for trespassers to advertise their presence. 'Please don't concern yourself, dear boy,' he drawled, 'but read this'. He took from his wallet a much folded piece of paper. It bore the Lion and Crown crest of the British Transport Commission, was headed 'General Manager's Office' and carried the following message: ALLOW CAPTAIN W.L. KENNING TO ENTER ANY SIGNAL BOX AND TO TRAVEL ON ANY ENGINE. It was signed, authentically, by a very high-ranking Western Region Officer and so, far from trespassing, Bill had every right to be in the box and therefore was *obliged* to sign the register to mark the length of his visit. I discovered later that Bill's son, Michael, had gone to his father's old school, Radley, and while there had been close friends with the son of the Very High Ranking Official's son.

Bill's enthusiasm for railways was equalled by his love of cricket — each year he arranged for the MCC to come to play Ditchling on the village green — and by his detestation of magpies and crows. It was this that caused him to carry those chimney-sweeping rods. He detested these particular birds because they ate the eggs of other birds so he conducted a war against the predators. When he saw a magpie's nest he stopped his car and planted his special, warning sign in the roadside verge. The sign was a red disc on a 5-ft-tall, white post. Across the middle of the disc was the word DANGER in white letters and all around the edge the words MAG-CROW OPERATIONS. He assembled his rods and advanced to the attack. When he had succeeded in dislodging the nest or nests he put them on the back seat of the car rather like a Red Indian brave adding another scalp to his belt. So this was Bill Kenning. He came often and at first I gave him step-by-step instructions as to how to answer a bell and pull a lever. It was only after he died that I discovered that he was well known in signal boxes from Brighton to Weymouth and Banbury and had, as an amateur, been working lever frames since 1913 at least. In all the time I knew him and told him how to do the job his courteous manners were such that he never said to me 'I know' but had simply accepted my instructions.

I did my own fair share of signal box visiting. The men on duty when I visited Didcot East Junction were Don Shackle and Joe Moore with a booking lad called Peter. Joe was from Devon, quite young for a Special Class signalman, but Don was perhaps sixty, tall and slim with an unaffectedly refined 'BBC English' accent. He worked in a railway jacket and waistcoat with a cloth cap. Joe spoke in loud, exuberant tones to 'the Lad', to Don and even to the passing trains, urging them to get a move on, whamming levers about with great vigour while Don worked quietly, with an economy of effort. When he passed Peter sitting on his tall stool at the booking desk and Peter tipped Don's cap over his eyes with the end of his ruler, Don would not raise his voice but would request gently, 'Try not to do that, Peter. I might trip over the cat.' I was never sure if Don's was an elegant and continuous piece of sarcasm or whether that was his real nature. There were several cats in the signal box. The Chief was 'old Tom', a black and white moggy who reclined on the instrument shelf or wandered casually amongst the instruments while they were being operated, draping his tail across the signalman's eyes. Another of his pleasures was to weave sinuously around the levers, threading his body through the gaps as levers were being slammed back into the row with the rest. He was quite deliberate about this as if he enjoyed hearing the Devonshire voice of Joe hurling curses at him when a lever had to be stopped in full flight to save the cat from being crushed. The other cats were the nursing mothers and their litters; one lived in a sack of waste paper at the east end of the 120-lever signal box and the other was in the locking room below the operating floor.

The first time I went into East Junction, Don said, in his quiet way, 'Are you interested in learning this job, Adrian?' He seemed most solicitous and I replied that I would like nothing better. 'Righto, then. There's an engine on the Newbury branch for shed. You can pull off for it.' He pressed the button on the loud-hailing Tannoy telephone which had a loudspeaker in the shunters' cabin. 'Clear the spur for one off the Gold Coast for shed,' he ordered. I was examining the track diagram over the instruments trying to see which levers unlocked which other levers; there seemed to be a great deal of pulling and pushing required and I had no idea where to start. After a minute the Tannoy crackled, 'OK, Don, clear on the Spur.'

'Come on then,' said Don, 'let's have that engine over.'

I had to admit defeat. 'Tell me what to pull and I'll pull them.'

Joe and Peter laughed and looked on with interest as Don began calling out the relevant lever numbers. Facing point bolts and the bolts on the switch diamonds had to be moved, and point levers pulled over and then re-bolted. The signal levers then had to be pulled. I thought I was never going to stop, especially as, being completely unfamiliar with the feel or weight of each lever, I did not know how hard to pull each one nor how easily each would come over. I pushed and pulled about thirty levers until, with a block of eighteen standing over in the centre of the frame, I had the route set and, with a cheeky 'toot', a little pannier tank came scampering diagonally across all the tracks to the down avoiding line goods loop where it stopped. Now that route had to be restored — thirty lever movements — and a fresh route set to the shunting spur and then into the engine line.

To assist the signalmen at Didcot East Junction and Reading West Main signal boxes in the organisation of the train services over their complicated and important junctions and to allow them to know how much time they could allot to shunting movements on or across the main lines, an instant information service between the two boxes was provided by the booking lads using a Tannoy. The 'send' button at Didcot East Junction was pressed and the booking lad would chant such messages as, 'Worcester up the runner, Swindon up the shute and the Weston's fifteen late off Swindon.' This blared out inside West Main box so that the Lad there noted it in the register and the signalmen knew that they could expect the Worcester express in thirteen minutes, the Swindon 'stopper' on the up relief line in twenty-five and the Weston, well, she was 'well down the pan' and they'd probably get the Swansea up first. The Tannoy was a loudspeaker system, not a telephone, and messages were interspersed with a fair amount of good-natured obscenity between the booking boys. Someone suggested that it would be a good idea if the Tannoy circuit could be extended to Steventon, then inquiries for train-running information — previously directed at Didcot East Junction from Swindon — could be re-directed to Steventon where the signalman had more time to deal with them. No one thought about the other part of the Tannoy broadcasts so that, when it was installed in Steventon box, right in the middle of the village, the raucous arguments of the booking lads at East Junction and West Main brayed out over the peaceful thatch and gardens where villagers sunned themselves in deckchairs. The Steventon signalmen were embarrassed, the villagers were outraged and, recovering themselves, the latter stormed the Station Master's office at Didcot and demanded that the objectionable thing be removed. It was.

Booking lads were sometimes a sore trial to their signalmen. Not from any failing on their part to do the job, on the contrary, all booking boys I ever came across were experts and, at sixteen years of age, were quite capable of doing the signalman's job for him. No, it was a highly competent, confident lad's appetite for mischief that could bear down heavily on the signalman. When Joe and Don could not see their lad they became nervous and looked about with feelings of mistrust, saying things like, 'Where's that blasted Peter got to?' And well they might. One day Joe went outside to kick back to 'Danger' a ground signal which had 'stuck off'. Don then had the entire box to manage and was too busy to notice Peter sliding back the west end window with one hand whilst holding a milk bottle full of water in the other. As Joe came back to the box he got a pint of cold water over his head and came roaring up the stairs vowing vengeance but Peter had already climbed into the rafters. Joe prodded at him with the broom handle but Peter refused to come down, hopping about on the beam, dodging the stick until, with the train register being neglected, Joe had to promise not to murder him if he came down. Through all this Don was patiently working the box and seeing to the register as best he could.

After a few minutes, Peter apologised and offered Joe a cigarette. Joe, mollified, took one, Peter had one too and asked

Joe for a light. Joe took out his box of Swan Vestas, lit up and handed the still burning match to Peter. The lad lit his cigarette and shoved the still-burning match into the box which Joe was holding in his hand. The box of matches ignited, Joe flung it away so that it landed on the cat who leaped onto the instrument shelf whilst Peter took once more to the rafters. Joe raced the length of the box to stamp on the burning box and all the while the imperturbable Don Shackle walked up and down his 120 levers, peaked cap facing sternly forwards, avoiding cat, boy and burning matchbox to answer bells and pull levers to keep the all-unsuspecting Great British Public on the move.

CHAPTER TWO

SCRAPPING STEAM

The semaphore system of signalling allowed men to feel free, to laugh and joke with mates on the telephone and, in signal boxes where there was a booking lad, to indulge in horseplay that could occasionally become rough. On the other hand, some signalmen were exceedingly strict with their lads. One man I particularly recall at Swindon would not allow his lad to spend more than thirty seconds in answering a telephone. Once, when I was walking along the track in the vicinity of the box, the booking lad came to the window to speak and was pulled back to his stool by the signalman! These are rarities, few boxes had booking lads and for the most part the job went along in good spirits. Between Foxhall Junction, Didcot, and Highworth Junction, Swindon, both boxes included, there were eleven signal boxes. In them were employed about forty-five signalmen with perhaps six Signal & Telegraph Department linemen for their maintenance. The 23 miles of track between Foxhall and Highworth Junctions were divided into 'block sections' with an average length of two miles. It may be said, therefore, that an express train was examined by a signalman every two or three minutes of its journey. The trains – passenger and freight – were shepherded along the route and any trouble was pounced on before it could develop into anything serious. Scores of men were usefully employed in serving the community; this was the railway I had known all my life and an excellent system it appeared to be. The equipment we used was relatively reliable, having stood the test of time over generations in some cases. During the period 5 September/7 October 1959 there was one track-circuit failure and one bell failure each lasting 90 minutes at Challow box; no other failure was logged in the train register during that time when at least 5700 trains passed the box. Between 29 April and 10 June 1964, when 'the writing was on the wall', Challow box suffered one equipment failure each week, with about 5500 trains passing the box in that time.

When I discovered that the signal box, which I so carefully polished and which I tried to be so conscientious in running, was considered by Management to be inefficient and that my mates and I were too expensive to employ I felt, not unnaturally, considerable inner turmoil. In 1963 nothing less than a revolution was under way. I saw the 'Western' and 'Hymek' diesels as the tumbrils, colour-light signals as gallows and top Management-types as the Dantons and Robespierres of the piece, busy guillotining old hands and dispensing with a large part of the railway — a way of life. The basis of my entire growing-up was being swept away; my loyalties were outraged and economics had no part of the argument. I wanted to live and work with all my mates and to digest bread, not balance sheets.

Had it not been for the much-maligned steam engines, Western Region could not have run a full service of trains, at times, between 1962–5. Some trains suffered three or four diesel failures on one journey before a steam engine came to the rescue. During the same period, scrapyards, both public and privately owned, could not keep up with the spate of steamers arriving at their gates for destruction while the factory at Swindon could not cope with the number of broken-down diesels awaiting repair. During 1963 the programme of diesel building was suspended in order to devote time to overhauling steam engines! Queues of scrap steam engines lined the trackside at Oxford, Didcot and Reading while queues of broken-down diesels waited for shops. Only the former gave rise to offence in the eyes of top Management and the decree went forth that steam engines had to be stored, hidden from public gaze.

There were on Western Region, on 1 November 1963, 247 condemned steam engines; thirty-nine were allocated to Swindon works for cutting-up but the remainder had to be sold to contractors. These private firms bought in bulk but could take only four or five engines a week as it required that time to break them and make room for more so that the total scrapping rate for Western Region was fifty per month with 1384 locomotives (not to mention hundreds of carriages and wagons) to be destroyed; the Region hoped to get the fleet down to 650 steam engines by the end of 1964. For me, this programme — however rational to Management — was nothing less than a wholesale slaughter of my 'best friends'. It also led to fewer trains being run, especially seasonal extras, which led to more mayhem on the roads. From October 1963 the pressure was on to get rid of steam engines even faster by finding fresh outlets — new scrapyards — and to 'improve the aesthetic appearance of some locomotive depots'* in the meantime by hiding the poor, rusting hulks from public gaze. In general the engines were scrapped on ex-GWR territory for the very good reason that there was a danger of the locomotives coming into contact with bridges and platform edges if they went 'abroad'. Some 'County' class engines were sent successfully to Norwich but when, in October 1963, Western Region sold 'Castle' class 5001, 5060, 7015 and 7037 to a firm in Blackwall on the Eastern Region the engines were en route before some ordinary railwayman questioned whether they would clear the Eastern Region loading gauge in that backwater of London's railway. Then the fat was in the fire! The breakers had paid for the engines as representing so many tons of this or that metal and the only way they could arrive at their destinations was if their cabs, chimneys, safety valves and outside cylinders were removed — the cost of dismantling being borne by Western Region. A period of reflection followed after which the breakers received five small tank engines and a credit note.

Firms buying many of the engines frequently came up against the problem of non-delivery. Several weeks after a firm had paid for an engine they discovered that it had not arrived

* Letter from London Divisional Manager to Chief Mechanical Engineer.

in their yard. On investigating this, Western Region found that such engines had been dispatched from the engine shed so there was a mystery until it was realised that the engines were travelling without name or number plates, these having been stripped off for sale to souvenir hunters; the breakers had no idea what had been delivered and what had not. It also appeared that engines were being towed to yards without so much as a waybill as a means of identification. The latter problem was solved by a few anguished letters from Head Office to the Divisions, and the matter of identity was solved with some white paint. The 'dead' engines ran without much regard for lubrication so coupling and connecting rods were removed and thrown into the tender — or 'coal department' as one scrapyard called it in a letter to Western Region. This enabled the engines to arrive with the right amount of white metal in the rods' bearings but then the breakers complained that some engines were arriving without any rods at all. It transpired that these were tank engines whose rods had been placed in the tender of another engine. Sometimes the condemned engines were hauled too fast and developed hot axle bearings whereupon the white metal ran onto the sleepers to the chagrin of the scrappers. One of the saddest sights, for me, was to see a condemned engine, in steam, hauling four or five of its brethren 'dead' to the knacker's yard.

There seems little doubt that serviceable engines were scrapped. As one diesel could, in theory, do the work of three steam engines, one new diesel to a depot would displace that many steamers and I think it is probable that many engines, recently repaired, were sent for scrap because of such displacement. Engines were condemned at a depot and sold to a scrap dealer at a price including transport from that depot to the scrapyard. There were cases where, after an engine had been sold for scrap, it was used in traffic and 'disappeared'. The scrap dealer would complain of non-delivery and the engine would be 're-discovered' at another depot a hundred miles away. What concerned the Region was the cost of getting the engine to the scrapyard, this being greater from the new site than that budgeted for a month earlier from the original depot. What concerned the Shed Foreman was finding enough engines to work the traffic; he would see a decent engine on 'death row' and borrow it. The knowledge that serviceable engines were being sent for scrap at a time of locomotive shortages must have been very frustrating to the operators. Sometimes, before an engine was sent away, its serviceable tender would be removed and replaced by an unserviceable one off a working locomotive. This would be detected by the scrapyard and a complaint lodged. Late in 1962 the Locomotive Department fought this issue with Head Office at Paddington; there was no reason why the scrapyard should want a 4500-gallon tender with a vacuum brake cylinder in good condition when that cylinder was needed for a working engine — there was just as much metal in a 4500-gallon tender with a defective vacuum brake cylinder. After a month of wrangling the point was conceded and tenders were authorised to be swapped.

That other piece of official tomfoolery, emanating from the General Manager, that scrap steam engines should be hidden from public gaze, led to a lot of wasted time, fuel and temper. On 27 November 1963 there were seventeen 'dead' engines, removed from public gaze, stored on sidings in Old Oak Common engine shed. By 12 December there were twenty-seven. The shed at that time was in process of being reconstructed as a 'diesel depot' and the alterations had placed siding space at a premium, the scrap engines were crowding working engines out of their legitimate siding space but complaints from the Chief Mechanical Engineer went without response. The situation was exceedingly difficult; in any case, the General Manager's directive simply exacerbated the situation. The engines were quietly taken back to Reading, Didcot and Oxford.

While the only reliable motive power Western Region possessed was being destroyed as fast as humanly possible, the pioneers of the new image — the diesels — were frequently breaking down. No one, not even I, would have suggested that the new traction was not immensely fast and powerful, but I was astonished at its apparent fragility: at £100,000 each surely such locomotives should have had the same measure of reliability as an equivalent steam engine costing one-tenth of that price to build? As it was, I was able to enjoy the sight of a steam engine in full cry at the head of an express train, standing in for some broken-down diesel, being driven with great gallantry by a crew determined to show what a real engine could do. Gradually, but inexorably, the diesels took over more trains until, by the start of September 1963, all Cheltenham, Bristol, Worcester, South Wales and West of England expresses were scheduled for diesel haulage. On 24 September the Bristol Division issued a notice to all staff regarding the lack of punctuality, which concluded: 'The seriousness of the position is reflected in the fact that, compared to the corresponding period last year, there was a decrease of nearly 13% in the number of passenger trains arriving at their destination on time and in addition more than 10% arrived 30 minutes late or more.' It seemed to me, at the time, useless to complain to the men about a lack of punctuality when it was the Management's Gadarene approach to the 'modern image' that was resulting in bad time-keeping.

On 27 September the Worcester line was back to 100 per cent steam haulage as its 'Hymeks' either failed or were taken for use on more important routes. Goods trains were cancelled to provide diesel power for express trains and Swindon factory was ordered to suspend its new diesel-building programme to concentrate on clearing the backlog of diesel repairs and to repair more steam engines. The latter were given medium attention, falling short of new or exchange boilers or cylinders. They were turned out in fresh, GWR-type livery to give employment to boilersmiths and other craftsmen who were otherwise redundant in the diesel age. I believe I am correct in writing that, on 27 September 1963, there were thirty-five failed diesels in Swindon factory, two at Didcot shed and nine at Old Oak Common. No doubt lines of broken-down diesels did not offend the eye of our General Manager and the travelling public and perhaps the latter did not mind being delayed for upwards of an hour so long as the source of the delay was a 'modern image' at the head of their train — but I was furious, for all the time 'my' steam engines were being slandered as 'inefficient' whilst they continued to prop up the railway system.

Although Swindon was turning out some very capable, very smart, 'Hall', 'Grange', and 'Manor' class engines, among other types, it was not always these that were to be seen at the head of express passenger trains. I recall seeing, on 9 March 1964, 4089 *Donnington Castle* with the up 'Cathedrals Express' at Oxford. The engine had been 'stored' for a year or so and had corroded to a ghastly, corpse-like green. It carried neither name nor number plates and had no glass in any of the cab windows. There was a bitter wind blowing so the crew were working in atrocious conditions but they had done their passengers proud. A ten-minute late start from Kingham, arising from the earlier diesel failure, had been cut to a five-minute late start from Oxford, and Paddington was reached five minutes early; this was on the diesel's accelerated schedule with a load of 420 tons. I wonder if anyone complained about the 'scrap' engine at the head of their train? I wonder even more if anyone bothered to thank the enginemen for their splendid effort?

On 1 May 1964, following complaints from Worcester line passengers regarding the lack of modern motive power on their line, efforts were made to re-dieselise them. On 3 May the 'Hymek' on the 4.5 p.m. Hereford failed at Norton Junction, just south of Worcester, and 6960 *Raveningham Hall** was substituted. None of the passengers got out and walked as far as I am aware. 6960 *Raveningham Hall* left Norton Junction 32 minutes late with nine coaches for 320 tons and arrived in Paddington six minutes late. In October 1964 the down 'Cathedrals Express' failed at Finstock Halt, 5 miles beyond Handborough, 1½ miles before Charlbury, causing a delay of 2½ hours. In fairness to the 'Hymek' all the delay was not

* Now privately owned in first-class working order on Severn Valley Railway.

attributable to its malfunction — the 'secondman' walked back to Handborough for assistance rather than forwards to Charlbury. Assistance took the form of a much-despised steam engine, 73049, from Oxford shed. This shoved the train through to Kingham where it was able to get onto the front of the train and, hauling the 'dead' diesel and its train, kept the schedule to Worcester.

At Challow I saw a good deal of 'ex-works' steam engines because, as they came from the shops, the Swindon Shed Foreman put them onto the traditional 'running-in' turn on the Challow 'stopper'. In 1964 this was the 7.35 a.m. Swindon to Didcot, first stop Challow. The load was two coaches and many men used the job to have a merry dash up the main line. I kept a daily record of their exploits when I was on early turn and logged some hilarious sprints, far faster than was required by the timetable. The motive power was provided by the 'Modified Halls', 'Granges' and 'Manors', all looking spick-and-span in their livery of middle chrome green. They braked to 20 mph for the junction points from up main to up relief some 300 yards before the signal box and then opened up hard, accelerating past the box before screeching to a stand at the station. The drivers knew I was interested in their games and always had a smile and a wave for me as they shot past the signal box. On 31 January 1964, 7928 *Wolf Hall* went from Swindon to Challow station, start to stop, $13^{1}/_{8}$ miles, in 13 minutes and, it should be remembered, the driver had to come down to 20 mph half a mile before the station. On 22 February 7928 *Wolf Hall* was hauling the 10.5 a.m. Hereford, 320 tons, 50 minutes late starting from Oxford as a result of a diesel failure. Paddington was reached 36 minutes late with a steady 92 mph over the 14 miles from Maidenhead to Southall. That was showing them how! I was on board and felt so proud of the engine and the men who were willing to have a go.

The story of the closure of Challow station has already been told in *Signalman's Twilight*. Western Region Management simply saw the place as a complication, an extra stop, a 'bump' on the otherwise station-less railway between Didcot and

Swindon. The fact that Challow had been a successful passenger station and was ideally sited in a wide, rural area to act as what is now known as a 'Parkway' was of no importance. Local railwaymen pointed this out to Wantage Town Council and urged that a station be kept at either Challow or Wantage but no one seemed interested. During the last twenty years, however, the district has grown in importance and a completely new road system has had to be built from Steventon and Didcot to carry growing numbers of commuters from the Vale to Didcot station. The cost of this road, though it comes from taxpayers' money, is not shown on the railway balance sheet and no one asks whether roads are profitable.

Bill Kenning and Ron Price came to Challow to help local people and staff give the last train — the 6.1 p.m. Didcot to Swindon, hauled by 6112 — a decent send-off with every fog signal 'banger' we had in stock.

Since Challow was shut on 5 December 1964, Western Region has subsequently opened 'Parkway' stations at Castle Cary, Bristol and near Tiverton. Perhaps they might, after all, reopen 'Challow Parkway'?

After the station's closure all that remained was the signal box standing rather forlornly beside the line and, snaking alongside the rails, the black cables, the tentacles of Reading Panel signal box, reaching out 30 miles to strangle the signal boxes of the Vale and Thames Valley. As a fully paid-up member of the 'Luddite Brotherhood' I could see no virtue in the new system of signalling. It would cost £1,500,000 to put 200 men out of work, run fewer trains (the service had decreased drastically with modernisation) and serve fewer stations. Furthermore, as far as I was concerned, it was not such a safe system as the old; I might have been wrong in this, but that is how I felt.

In earlier times the railway was relatively free of hot axle-boxes. This is an emergency when a wagon or carriage axle, turning on its bearing in the axle box, runs short of lubrication as a result of neglect or due to an oil-film breakdown from overloading or excess speed. In any case the axle end soon becomes red-hot and, if left unattended, will shear off and put the wagon down on the track. In the train register from Shrivenham signal box for the period 18 July to 22 August 1958, when at least 6000 trains passed the box, there were no instances of hot axle-boxes recorded. In the Challow train register for the period of 5 September to 8 October 1959, when approximately 5700 trains passed, there was one instance of a 'hot box' recorded but between 13 and 18 May 1965 there were six 'hot boxes' out of about 650 trains. Only the presence of a signal box every two or three miles prevented a serious accident; a signalman would see the crippled bearing and take steps not only to have that train stopped but also to prevent any other train from passing the cripple while it was moving.

When Reading Panel became fully operational the men there controlled — if that is the right word — the tracks as far west as Challow. The first semaphore signalling signal box was at Uffington. Thus trains ran from Scours Lane, Reading, to Moreton Cutting, Didcot — about 15 miles — without any manually controlled signal to stop them should they be running in a dangerous condition or to bring them to a stand should some other train have become derailed. Having been brought up on the old system it filled me with alarm when contemplating this expensive shambles. Reading Panel extended its control to include Steventon on 27 September 1964. The up and down relief lines between Wantage Road and Challow were taken out of use on 4 April 1965 and on 26 May Challow lost its crossover points leaving only double-track main line and a number of de-armed signal posts. There were two vacancies for signalmen at Uffington box and three redundant signalmen at Challow: Jim Spinage, Ken Rowlands and myself. I was by far the most junior so there seemed no chance of my going to Uffington but around 26 May Ken Rowlands decided against continuing on the railway. Uffington would be abolished in two or three years so he felt he might as well get out while he was that much younger. This meant I was given the last vacancy at Uffington. My last shift in Challow box was the early turn on Saturday 29 May 1965 and at 3 p.m. the following day I was present in the box with Ken and Jim to hear a ceremonial 'Closing Signal Box' code, 7-5-5 on the bell, sent to Wantage Road and Uffington by Ken Rowlands who had begun his career on the Great Western, in Challow box, as a booking lad — and a very conscientious one, too, apprenticed to that most meticulous of signalmen, Bert Snell.

I did not go immediately to Uffington. Much to my surprise I was told to stay at Challow, booking on there each day, to watch the trains go by and report on the telephone to Uffington if I saw anything amiss. Poetic justice, perhaps — I was so concerned about the lack of supervision of trains! The poetry of the situation had lost its savour by Wednesday. I telephoned the Staff Office to ask when I could go to Uffington and was told to hang on for a few more days. On Friday, alarmed at the thought of being forgotten at Challow, I telephoned again. On this occasion, the man at the opposite end of the wire in Reading thought he was talking to his colleague in Bristol and, when I asked to go to Uffington, said something to the effect, 'Well, you know what the trouble is, the District Inspector doesn't want him there.' The Swindon D.I. had known me since I was eleven and had passed me on the rules for Uffington and Challow. I expressed a certain surprise at the Staff Officer's announcement and the man I was talking to, covered in confusion when he realised who he was talking to, told me to report for work at Uffington the following Monday morning.

CHAPTER THREE

CAUSE FOR CONCERN

Jim showed me the workings and the equipment of the new Uffington that Monday morning, his voice increasingly showing his concern as he went on. It was the lack of control over the signals that worried both of us most. Once a train left the area of controlled signals at Uffington, Didcot or Reading it was 'on its own' for 10–15 miles; there was always a signal showing red for 'Danger' behind the train but there was no manually controlled signals in those long sections which could be manually placed to 'Danger' to stop trains in the case of a derailment or other emergency. This seemed to us — Jim, Elwyn and me — to be a major failing in the new system of Multiple Aspect Signalling (MAS) but the system was sacred — the latest, money-saving idea — and to criticise it on any account was to bring one's own sanity into question. The other great problem at that time was the sheer unreliability of the equipment. Diesel engine failures had long since become commonplace. The system was 'fail-safe' but that did not make delays from track-circuit failures, signal post telephone failures and berserk automatic lifting barriers any the less annoying. The malfunctions of the instrument used to 'describe' trains between Reading Panel and Uffington would have been funny had they not been such a nuisance. I spent five mornings with Jim, learning what I had let myself in for, with the suspicion growing that the entire installation had been rushed through — like dieselisation — so as to make Western Region the first, wholly modernised Region of British Railways. It was up to the men to try and keep it working.

The lever frame at Uffington had been renewed in 1962 to operate the Faringdon branch and the newly laid up and down goods loops each of which held 80 wagons plus the engine and

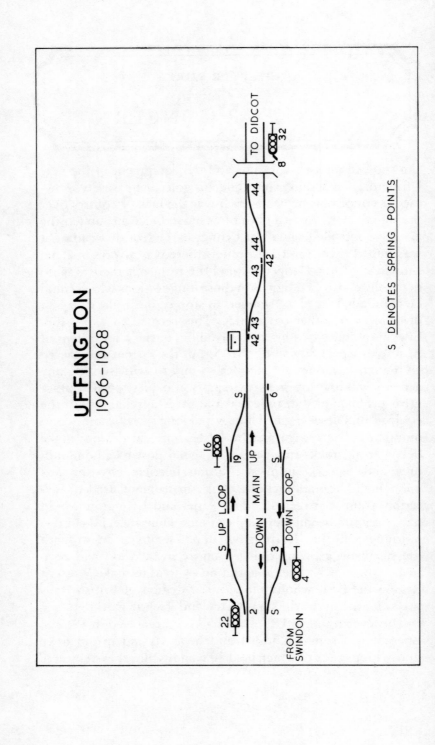

UFFINGTON
1966 - 1968

S DENOTES SPRING POINTS

brake van. By May 1965 the branch was shut and although there were 47 levers in the frame only 15 were working. They were ranged along the back wall of the box, leaving a clear view of the tracks from windows normally obstructed by levers and signalling instruments. This felt strange to work at first but it was a good idea and a further improvement was effected by locating the main-line signal levers directly below the signalling instruments. All the signals were colour-lights, so that, having carried out the signalling routine I could simply reach down and, with a light effort, pull over the required levers. Knighton Crossing signal box was still in use in June 1965 so the signal levers for signals at the east end of the layout were locked at 'Danger' until the signalman at Knighton gave a 'Line Clear' indication on the instrument. On the up line the signals were switched from red to yellow and then green as the preceding train moved away eastwards; all I had to do was pull the lever over. The points at the exit from the down goods loop and at the entrance to the up loop, 1000 yards away to the west, were worked by electric motors when I moved the lever but those at the east end of the loops, close to the box, were operated manually through levers and rodding.

On the instrument shelf there was the traditional block bell and instrument for working to Knighton. This worked perfectly but the 'train describer', by which train identification codes were sent and received between Uffington and Reading Panel, was broken down as often as it was operational. Each train had an identification code — 1C75, for instance, for the 12.30 p.m. Paddington to Penzance express — and that number moved along the console that was Reading Panel as the train moved over the ground. As the 12.30 p.m. Paddington passed the down goods loop at Steventon its number came into my describer. Each digit had to click into place in the bottom display box — 1C75 was 16 loud clicks — followed by an infernal squawking as the 'Acknowledge' button flashed and demanded to be pressed. Having been pressed in, the number then ascended through five display boxes, clattering into each before setting out for the next — 90 maddening clicks. Luckily the buzzer had to be silenced only once which to my biased mind was an oversight on the part of the designer. The machine was so irritating that the three Uffington signalmen often became convinced that it actually enjoyed going through its rigmarole and made its silly noise merely to be spiteful. If I was lucky it would go wrong, fill itself up with 0Z00 numbers and thereafter remain silent until someone could find the time to mend it; in the meantime the signalman at Uffington and the Panelman at Reading worked with the traditional, single-strike bell.

One night, soon after I started work at Uffington, the describer showed 5T25 — 12.5 a.m. Paddington to Cardiff express goods — coming down with 1B00 — 2.15 a.m. Paddington to Bristol newspapers — right behind. I set the points for the down goods loop and waited for the goods to appear under Baulking bridge. After a few minutes I saw the lights of a train standing at the bridge and the 'Call' light began flashing to show that someone was phoning in from signal 8/32. I answered the call and a voice said, 'You've got us going into the loop.'

'Yes, that's right — the 2.15 Padd. is close behind you.'

'We *are* the 2.15 Padd. You want to get your sleep before you come to work.'

The phone went dead. I put the lever back, re-set the route and pulled off again. A couple of minutes later a 'Warship' diesel came roaring down, the driver flashing the cab interior light on and off as he approached. 5T25 was following behind so both trains were delayed and, as expected, both drivers blamed me. What had happened was that, as the description 1B00 moved alongside 5T25 on the console at Reading — the goods being in the loop at Steventon — the electrical circuitry transposed the numbers and thus misled me. Once we became aware of this tendency we tried to look out for clues to make sure that the describer was not misleading us and were then caught out less often.

Naturally, there were human errors. When an up train was approaching Uffington I dialled its number into the 'Set Up' box and, as the train passed, pressed the 'Send' button. I forgot to press the button one day and, having dealt with the train, forgot about it, it was off my patch. After a while Reading Panel rang to say there was a track circuit failure on the up line at Steventon. Two minutes later the Panelman rang again.

'You know I said we had a track down at Stivvy?'

'Yes.'

'Well, it's just rung up to say it's the 9.20 Severn Tunnel. Pull your finger out.'

Track circuit failures, real or false, were potentially danger-ous in the situation that existed between Reading and Uffing-ton. The failure will hold the signal to the rear of the failure at 'Danger' and thus, when a train comes to a stand at that signal, its driver will be told to pass it at 'Danger' because it is only at 'Danger' as the result of a failure of equipment. But if it was not a failure, but rather an unreported train standing on the track you had the chance of a rear-end collision. One morning at Uffington I had a total power failure and the stand-by generator did not work. There was a train standing at every signal on my patch and not a signal post telephone working. The last signal on Reading Panel's patch was held at 'Danger' by the presence ahead of a train standing at the first signal on my section. A train came to a stand at Reading's last signal and its driver telephoned to the Panel for instructions. The Panel-man could not contact me because the phones had failed, so he told the driver to go by the signal — 'probably only a track failure' [there were so many] and to go on cautiously. Unfortu-nately the driver was not quite as cautious as he might have been and very nearly ran into the back of the train in front. I know because he told me so when he finally reached Uffington and stopped to ask what all the delay was about. Men became impatient of all the failures and consequential delays.

Sheer, unmitigated impatience accounts for the next tale. My down goods loop starting signal was a three-aspect colour-light; it had three lenses to show red, yellow or green but, while Knighton Crossing signal box was in use, the yellow aspect was not connected and it could show only red or green like the semaphore signal it had replaced. One morning I had a goods train waiting in the loop and the driver had expressed a certain restlessness to be on his way. After the third and final express of the 'string' had passed, I set the points for the goods to leave and stood by the instruments ready to 'get the road' as soon as the 'fast' cleared Knighton. This I duly did but found the loop starting signal lever locked in the frame. Puzzled, I checked that I had indeed got a 'Line Clear' indication, then checked the track circuits. The one in advance of the loop, out on the down main line towards Knighton, was showing 'occupied' — which would lock the signal in the loop — and for a moment I thought I had a track-circuit failure until I saw that the red light indicating the presence of the goods train in the loop had gone out. I whirled round to look out of the window. The loop was empty and, just disappearing, a mile away, was the brake van of the goods. If I had seen the illegal movement taking place I would have sent the 'Train running away' bell — 4.5.5 — to Knighton but now the train had the road and I was unsure what to do about it. I telephoned Chris Midwinter at Knighton: 'Don't pull off for that goods, Chris, stop it and ask the driver to come on the phone.

A few minutes later the driver was asking grumpily, 'Wassa-matter?'

'What aspect did you have when you left my loop?'

'A yellow, of course,' he replied truculently.

'Cheeky beggar. That signal can show only red or green. You went past it at "Danger".'

'Well, you'd set the road for me,' he growled. 'What are you going to do about it?'

'Nothing,' I replied cheerfully. 'I just wanted you to know that you would have looked pretty silly if that down fast had stopped while you were charging down the main behind it.'

Drivers very occasionally passed a signal at 'Danger' through an unintentional oversight but I had never, in years of listening to other men's anecdotes, heard of an instance where a driver did so deliberately and I never came across another case. In a world of changing technology and changing values the railwaymen did their best to preserve their integrity, often in the face of a rather demoralising situation. Punctuality — arriving at work ten minutes before the appointed hour — continued to be observed as far as possible. Jim Spinage relieved me at 6 a.m. on one occasion, bursting into the box, apologising for being late with cow muck all down his overcoat. He had been a minute or two behind schedule and had driven his scooter rather faster than usual around the turning from the Uffington–Baulking lane into the Station Road. The machine was leaning well to the right when the front wheel encountered a deep deposit of green goo recently laid by a herd of cows on their way to milking. Elwyn Richards was badger-like in his habits. Since 1943 he had walked the mile and a half from Uffington village to the station, through the gate and over the footbridge; whatever the weather, Elwyn, with his gas-mask case and carrying his lunch over his shoulder, would be on time. Every day Mrs MacBayne, who was landlady of the Junction Hotel put a pint of stout through the hedge at the back of the down platform for his lunch or tea and, at the end of a late turn, at 10 p.m., Elwyn would go into the pub to fortify himself for the walk home. So regular was this observance that Mrs MacBayne had the stout poured and waiting on the bar before he arrived.

Elwyn was the man most strained by the constant alarms, failures and general eccentricities of work in Uffington signal box — eccentricities that became ever more bizarre from 27 November 1966 when automatic-lifting half-barriers replaced the manually controlled gates at Knighton and Ashbury Crossings. Because of our lack of control over signals we were obliged to allow trains to proceed towards dangerous situations. There were no 'controlled' signals to protect the previously mentioned level crossings, for instance, and when I complained to a Signal & Telegraph Department official he said: 'Accidents don't happen very often and we can't go to all that expense putting controlled signals along the line just to guard against the odd occasion.' On Western Region in 1965 there were 49 derailments. Throughout British Railways during 1965 there were a total of 80 derailments of freight trains on plain track.* No wonder, then, that we at Uffington were worried about the inadequacies of our signalling system. The Hungerford crash took place on 1 July 1965 on semaphore-signalled tracks but on a length where trains ran 8½ miles without signals to stop their progress. This was exactly the system I was complaining about with MAS, a system that had cost £1.5 million to instal.

On 1 July 1965 Driver Nokes of Westbury was driving D801 *Vanguard* hauling the 8.45 p.m. Exmouth Junction to Acton goods. As the train passed Savernake box at 3.40 a.m. the signalman saw an axle-box glowing red-hot on a 16-ton mineral wagon and sent the 'Stop & Examine' code — 7 bells — forward to Hungerford as Nokes took his train away into the night at a steady 40 mph. Three miles further on, 700 yards before passing Bedwyn signal box, the axle sheared from the wheel, the wagon dropped, both axles were torn from the body and in that condition the hulk was dragged over concrete-sleepered track until it was stopped by signals at Hungerford. By then it had destroyed 4½ miles of virtually new track and damaged another ¾ mile, left wheels obstructing the down line and smashed the parapet of a bridge. The crash caused five days of diversions, with much of the Hungerford line's West of England traffic running via Uffington. Additional delay was caused when the 'Salmon' class wagons carrying the new track became derailed at Hungerford but the double-track main line was finally re-opened on Monday 5 July. Bedwyn box was closed on night shift but open during the day. Had it been open that night the damage would have been confined to a few hundred yards and might have been avoided altogether. How many night-shifts could have been purchased for the cost of replacing the track and the cost of making all the diversions? What would have been the cost of a weighbridge at the quarry? At Merehead quarry 'weighing' was done by the Carriage & Wagon Examiner, who decided if

* See Appendix 3.

a wagon was overloaded by looking at the 'flatness' of each wagon's springs. Whoever he was, he was a skilful operator because incidents such as at Hungerford were few though one is enough, especially when trains were running for long distances unsupervised.

Early in September 1965 a midday parcels train ran on the down relief line from Tilehurst to Moreton Cutting, Didcot, 13 miles, with a four-wheeled van derailed at the rear. The van did not become uncoupled but danced from side to side of the track. Drivers of up trains, on seeing this, were naturally alarmed, braked to a stand and told the Reading Panelman in no uncertain terms what they thought of signalmen who allowed such things to happen. In fact there was nothing the Panelman could do until the train came to a stand at his first controlled signal — at Moreton Cutting. Early in November there was a similar incident when up trains stopped and their crews reported a hot axle-box on a petrol tanker. That the people in charge had allowed such a system to be installed — and at such cost in terms of employment — did nothing to improve our morale or our respect for those in charge.

On 5 November 1965, Guy Fawkes night, a spent rocket landed on signalling cables lying unenclosed on the ground near Old Oak Common. In a few minutes the cables had been burned through, destroying the entire signalling system in the Acton area at 7.50 p.m. No points would work, all signals were unlit. The 7.45 p.m. Paddington to Bristol was diverted at Old Oak Common to run via the Birmingham line to Greenford and thence southwards to join the Bristol line near Hanwell. Unfortunately for the passengers on the train, by the time they had completed their diversion and were approaching the Bristol main line, the fire had spread, wiping out all signalling between Old Oak and Southall. The procedure then was to run trains by the venerable 'time interval' system. All points were clipped and padlocked for straight running and trains passed from one hand-signalman to the next with extreme caution, each train following the first by a specified time interval. Under such conditions it was impossible to introduce a train into the main line from the branch because the whereabouts of potentially conflicting movements were unknown. The 7.45 p.m. Paddington remained trapped on the Greenford Loop until the Signal & Telegraph men, working flat out, restored some order. The train passed me at Uffington exactly three hours late at three minutes past midnight. In view of the difficulties involved in restoring communications this was good work but you should have heard the groans of disgust and exasperation from the signalmen when they were told about the failure — and the reason for it. As for the feelings of the passengers . . .

I was on night shift on 16 November and experienced three diesel failures in two hours. The 7.45 p.m. Paddington passed me two hours late, the original engine having suffered a total failure of its transmission system; the 9.30 p.m. Paddington's diesel failed at Reading and the 10.30 p.m. Paddington came limping past with its diesel sinking fast. Its driver had asked for a fresh engine at Reading but as he was the fourth man to make such a request that evening there were no spare engines nor any train available from which a diesel could be 'borrowed'. All this was fairly commonplace. Is it any wonder I was angry as I compared the much-vaunted new system with the old? It seemed to me that the Management did not know what was required to run a railway, only how to cut costs. It was as if the Great God of Modernisation had sent them mad or blind or both.

As 1965 drew to a close, foul weather began to batter our beleaguered Western Region. On 10 December, about 200 yards east of Bridgend station, close to the junction with the Vale of Glamorgan line, six tons of rock fell from the face of a cutting some 34 ft deep. It did not block the line but landed on the sleeper ends. The Engineering Department Inspector was called and, after examining the site, pronounced it safe. On the 12th the rock was carried away, the rockface checked and, again, pronounced safe. The cutting was through limestone sandwiched between clay, and past experience had shown that the rock outcrops tailed back into the hillside and were part of a solid mass. During the night of 16/17 December about 1½ in. of rain fell. At 5 a.m. on the 17th a 'light' engine passed up the main and the next train was 1Z60, 4 a.m. Carmarthen to Bristol, twelve empty coaches hauled by D1671. This passed Bridgend station, braking for a 50 mph permanent-speed restriction at 5.45 a.m. and at 5.47 ran headlong into a landslide of rock and clay from the site of the 10 November slip. Heavy rain had percolated down behind the cutting rockface and forced the rock and soil forwards, for at that particular spot the rock did not tail back into the hill.

As the coaches were tumbling across the down main and Vale of Glamorgan lines, D1671 was ploughing through the spoil and was struck head-on by D6983 hauling sixty empty wagons. Driver Ivor Ferrier of the 4 a.m. Carmarthen and his secondman, Donald Brock, were both killed. The site of the landslide was about 150 yards east of where Bridgend East signal box had stood until it was abolished under the Port Talbot MAS scheme in March 1965. It is probable that, had the signal box still been in use, the deaths would not have happened. Even if the signalman did not hear tons of rock falling 30 ft onto the track, his signal wires would have been struck violently which would have rattled the levers and, when he came to lower his up line signals, he probably would have not been able to pull his starting signal owing to the weight of spoil lying on it. Being aware of the earlier fall he would have put two and two together. It is not possible to be certain but the strong probability is there.

On that run-up to Christmas 1965 Western Region were gallantly trying to cater for the public and had scheduled extra passenger trains to run when the bad weather struck, hence the dislocation of services was worse than if the bad weather had occurred in, say, February. While the Bridgend job was being cleared, Chipping Sodbury tunnel became flooded so as to make it dangerous for diesel-electric locomotives to pass so all South Wales to London services were diverted via Gloucester until a landslide at Chepstow blocked that route and the entire service was re-routed via Chippenham and Stapleton Road,

Bristol, with South Wales passenger and freight trains all cramming into the one down main line and one up main line between North Somerset Junction and Didcot. Jim, Elwyn and I were daily and nightly very busy and, from my point of view, this at least was great fun (if that is the right word). By 22 December chaos reigned. Broken rails and floods and landslides combined with diesel failures in one glorious mess — including the ramming of the 4.30 p.m. Paddington by the following 'seasonal extra', the 4.35 p.m. Paddington. On 28 December the 8.30 a.m. Paddington to Plymouth was derailed just after it had left Reading, when it encountered a broken rail on the embankment high above the back gardens of Gower Street and later that day the 9.5 a.m. Severn Tunnel freight came off the road at Foxhall Junction, Didcot. Yet, in spite of it all, the men kept slogging away at the job, the trains continued to roar through Uffington and the passengers were, for the most part, taken successfully to their destinations.

CHAPTER FOUR

CLOSE ENCOUNTERS

There were forty derailments on British Railways in 1965, most of them on Western Region. In the first six weeks of 1966 Western Region suffered seven derailments. On 6 January 1966 I booked on at 10 p.m. in Uffington box for an eight-hour night shift. Some time before midnight I put a goods into the down loop to allow the 10.30 p.m. Paddington to Penzance sleeping car express to pass. As usual, the 'Sleeper' was followed closely by the 9.2 p.m. Acton to South Wales express freight so I held the goods in the loop for the Acton to pass. The driver of the slow goods in the loop was talking to me by phone from the loop starting signal when the Acton came storming under Baulking bridge, 400 yards to the east. The sound of a hammering 'Hymek' diesel burst into earshot as the train came through the arch and I put down the phone to watch as the engine's lights came into sight.

A trail of sparks was flying off the train, low down, close to the ballast. I looked hard for a moment to see if this phenomenon might be a hot axle-box, brakes dragging or something worse. It *was* worse. Even in the dark it was obvious that the rain of sparks was neither a flaming axle-box nor an iron brake-shoe striking or dragging against a wheel for a 'Catherine wheel' effect. It looked very much as if there was a wagon off the rails. Ahead of the train lay the diverging tracks at the points into the goods loop. It seemed as if I would very shortly have wagons flying left and right — and there was a guard sitting peacefully in the van at the rear of the train in the loop, only a few yards from the points. If the derailed wagon successfully negotiated the points then there was 2½ miles of track to rip up culminating in the tarmac road at Knighton, flush with the rails, which would surely smash the grounded wagon and derail all the others behind. These thoughts took no more than a second to go through my head. The longer the train ran on the greater would be the damage it caused. I pulled over the emergency detonator placer lever, threw the down starting signal to 'Danger' and ran to the window with the 'Bardic' electric torch to give the driver a red light. The 'Hymek' diesel was close to the box and I saw the driver's startled face lit blue-white for an instant in the flash from the exploding 'shots'. Seconds later flying ballast was rattling against the side of the box as a pair of long wheel-base wagons went ploughing through the sleepers, one at least without a pair of wheels. There was a crescendo of rattling ballast, smashing cast iron and splintering wood accompanied by the usual jangle of a passing freight train. Stepping quickly to the bell I sent 'Obstruction Danger', 6 bells, to Knighton Crossing and then thought of the driver of the train in the loop, patiently waiting on his phone, half a mile away, waiting for me to come back to him. I grabbed the telephone. He was whistling quietly to himself. 'Get down the bank,' I yelled into the mouthpiece. 'This one's off the road!' He stepped forward, unthinkingly, around the front of his own engine to see what was the matter and narrowly missed death under an avalanche of flying wood and steel. One 60-ft length of rail was discovered later out on the fields on the downside of the line.

The driver of the Acton braked steadily, with great skill and foresight, so that the train came to no more harm through wagons piling up over each other and came to a stand three-quarters of a train's length past my starting signal. I listened for the racket to cease, put the kettle on and telephoned Control for the breakdown gangs and crane. The first man into the box was the guard off the 9.2 p.m. Acton. He flung himself through the door, into the signal box, and straight down into the armchair. 'Sod this for a life,' he said with evident annoyance, 'that's the second time I've been off the road with this train. I was the guard when it came off at Steventon back in '62.'

It wasn't our day, clearly. That evening the 6.45 p.m.

Paddington's empty coaches were drawn into the station from Old Oak Common by the engine for the 7 p.m. Paddington. The engine for the 6.45 backed on but refused to change gear when asked, the driver could not get it into forward gear so it had to be 'failed'. This blocked-in the engine required for the 7 p.m. departure. The engine for a later departure was brought to haul the failed engine to Ranelagh Bridge yard and then returned to work the 6.45 away, leaving thirty minutes late and by so doing, releasing the engine for the 7 p.m. departure. Unfortunately this engine had failed as it stood against the buffers so another, later, service was robbed of its engine and the 7 p.m. left twenty-five minutes late. There was no doubt that, when the diesels ran, they were faster and more powerful than all but the biggest steam engines but, at a time when the steady performance of the steam engines was a vivid memory, the unreliability of these expensive diesels and the inconvenience this caused the passengers did irk me greatly. I think, as much as anything, it was the propaganda that hurt, the denigration of the old and the fulsome praise of the new. The new railway was 'sold' to the public as part of the 'white-hot cutting edge of technology' but those of us who had to work with it knew that the edges were rather blunt, and not particularly hot.

At the subsequent Inquiry into the crash I was criticised by one member of the Inquiry for stopping the derailed train. He reckoned I ought to have let it run as then less damage would have been done to the track. The notion that one ought not to stop a derailed train was a novel one, bearing in mind the cost of replacing each sleeper as the train crunches over them. I wondered if he had heard about the incident between Bedwyn and Hungerford; I wondered what indeed he knew about railway work; I wondered how he would have fared in Uffington box with a second to make a decision rather than a week to mull it over. All this flashed through my head even as the man was speaking and, given the bruised state of my mind at the general condition of the railway, my ire rose. 'If you had seen and heard what I saw and heard you would have done the same as I did,' I snapped. I do not think he was used to mere workmen shouting at him. He opened his mouth to speak, I glared at him and there were the makings of a first-class row when the man in charge of the Inquiry waved his colleague aside. 'Yes, yes,' he said testily, 'he was quite right to stop the train. May we please get on with the Inquiry?'

On Saturday, 22 January 1966, I parked my Morris 8 on the frozen ruts where once the neat, brick 'milk dock' had stood and hurried through the snow and bitter cold to the warmth and light of the signal box. Elwyn was then at the end of a twelve-hour shift and looked grey and ill.

'Rough night then, Elwyn?' I asked. 'Looks as if you've had one.'

'I dare say I do look rough, so does the driver on the Llandilo vacuum, too, I expect. We've 'ad a proper ol' set-to, take a look in the Book.'

I signed on in the train register and saw that at 3.49 a.m. Ted Blackall in Reading Panel had sent Elwyn 6 bells for a suspected derailment on the down line at Lockinge, 1½ miles west of Steventon. 'And look at this yere,' said Elwyn, in an aggrieved tone, stabbing a finger at the page, 'two vacuums on the up line, one just passing the box when I got the six bells and not a damn thing I could do about either of them. This *is* a rotten job and no mistake.'

The emergency had been discovered by George Strong, a long-serving, ex-GWR man acting as Crossing Keeper at Steventon Causeway. He had watched the 12.5 a.m. Paddington to Cardiff vacuum goods go past his post behind D1052 *Western Viceroy* and had heard a loud bang as a certain wagon passed over the road crossing. A trail of sparks proceeded westwards. George, being an experienced man, knew just what that meant but first went outside to check. In the snow there were the marks of wheels, first on one side of the rails, then on the other. He walked westwards about forty sleepers and the marks went on into the darkness where he could hear faintly the diminishing rattle of the train. He turned to hurry back to his cabin and was spurred on by the fact of the rattle stopping suddenly. Something was seriously wrong with the down goods. Ted Blackall sent the 'Obstruction Danger' to Elwyn, Elwyn replied with the 4-5-5, 'Train running away', and all three men standing, listening on the same telephone circuit, waited in considerable suspense to see if the up trains would pass safely by the derailed down train. No wonder poor old Elwyn looked grey!

While they were anxiously awaiting the fate of the men in the cab of the Llandilo vacuum, that train was running towards the derailment at 45 mph under clear signals. The men on the 12.5 a.m. Paddington were sitting in the cab of their stationary engine wondering why they had been stopped, thinking that the guard had put his brake on. After two minutes they got down and walked back along their train, only then discovering that some wagons were derailed and leaning towards the up main line. The train had broken into two parts, the vacuum brakes' pipes had been torn apart and this action had automatically brought the train to a stand. The two locomotivemen were then galvanised into action. The driver ran to find a signal post telephone so that he could warn Reading Panel while the secondman went to the engine to get detonators with a view to going westwards and placing them on the up line to warn trains and make them stop. The driver tried two signal post telephones but neither of them were working and before his fireman could get any 'shots' down the Llandilo vacuum came along and rattled past at 45 mph, missing the derailed wagon by a few inches.

According to the tale that came down the proverbial grapevine (the story up to now is quite correct) the driver of the Llandilo vacuum was given such a fright when he saw the wagons, apparently leaning across his path, looming up out of the darkness, that he had to be taken to hospital for treatment for severe shock. He and his mate had been lucky, Western Region had been lucky — again — but the signalmen at Reading and Uffington were very unhappy, wondering when the luck would run out and when something truly horrifying would happen as they stood by, powerless to prevent it. And there was an additional bone of contention: the secondman of every permanent-way gang had, since time immemorial, made a careful patrol of his 'length' daily but, since October 1965, this was reduced to an 'every other day' inspection on the grounds that modern track did not need such close and careful maintenance. For the same reason the old 'gangs' each looking after a 'length' — five men to five miles — were dispensed with in favour of a mobile team where eleven men could maintain 22 miles of track. Whatever the official reason given this looked to all of us as another reduction in safety standards in order to reduce costs.

The Patrolman for the Challow length phoned me from Challow ground frame one morning. 'That down goods has got a beautiful hot box, Adrian, you'll want to put him away.' I thanked him. The train was 2½ miles away, well out of sight of my signal which I put back to 'Danger' and then awaited the arrival of the train before altering the route from down main to down goods loop. Under normal circumstances the train would have run down the main to Swindon and the driver was expecting so to do. He did not slow up after passing the distant signal at 'Caution', believing that I would 'clear' the signal at any moment, and left it rather late to brake when he realised the signal was not going to change. Then he braked heavily, in the vernacular he 'slammed the lot in'. I heard a terrific, hollow, 'boom', looked up and saw a cloud of dust billowing out of the cutting — from a range of 600 yards — before I saw the engine. The 100-ton diesel stopped, or rather, decelerated without difficulty, the noise like someone beating a huge drum was the sound of three-score empty coal tubs, which did not have brakes, running heavily into the braking locomotive. I pulled the signal lever as the corner of a 'Western' class diesel appeared slowly around the side of the bridge, the driver gave a 'honk' on his horn and let his train freewheel onwards. He knew and I knew what that sound portended and he went on to make amends for his earlier haste by some very skilful driving.

As the wagons came under Baulking bridge I saw a black,

tar-tanker riding on its rear pair of wheels only, the leading buffers cocked up on the frame of another tar-tanker ahead. All the other wagons were empty coal tubs and these, in running forward, had thrown the great weight against the tank wagon forcing it to ride up onto the wagon in front. As the driver came level with me I pointed down the train and made the appropriate mime. He nodded grimly and, tensed-up, continued to concentrate on getting his train into the loop. The crisis would come when the wagons turned left and then right, over the 'S' shaped curve of the points from main to loop; as each turned there was a danger that the buffers lodged up on the other wagon would drop and the wagon's wheels would fall back to the track — but not onto the rails. I stood by the bell, watching the train's careful progress, waiting to send 'Obstruction Danger' the moment a derailment occurred. The driver, however, did not use any power; he allowed the train to freewheel into the loop, buffers closed up, and with sufficient energy in the train itself he was able to get into the loop without having to exert any traction which would almost certainly have pulled apart the locked-up wagons. It really was a fascinating exhibition of skill — and a little luck. The sequel was not so lucky. After the second tanker was rerailed the train was taken on to Swindon where the leading tar tank was found to have been punctured by the buffers of the other tank. The punctured tank was shunted onto a siding and the wind blew tar, like black threads, all over the train standing on the adjacent siding — a train-load of brand new cars.

Hot axle-boxes and a certain lack of signalling makes a poor outlook. Before 1963 there was no speed limit for freight trains on open track; they ran as fast as the driver's brake power permitted and as fast as the timetable required. A 'J' headcode train of empty tubs would have run at no more than 30 mph in steam days and an 'H' headcode train of coal would have run at around 25 mph; the criterion was brake power and being able to stop a heavy, unbraked train safely. A 'D' or 'C' headcode train, which was partly or fully vacuum braked, could run very much faster and did, making speeds of 50 mph. With

an increasing number of derailments on Western Region
(in particular) from April 1963 a maximum speed limit
of 55 mph for fully braked freight trains was imposed with
50 mph for all lesser trains. The number of derailments
caused by freight wagons continued to increase so in 1966 a
limit of 45 mph was placed on any train conveying wagons
with a wheelbase of 10 ft or less. Somewhat illogically, the
timetable was not altered to take account of the restriction,
maybe because if the timetable schedules were slowed down
this would have been an admission of the failure of modernisation. So the drivers had to run trains at an average start-to-stop
speed of 44.5 mph when they were not allowed to exceed 45
mph. There was obviously no margin to offset time lost in
reaching maximum speed and in decelerating, time lost in
signal checks, temporary restrictions over newly laid track.
The maximum speed restriction also meant that the men could
be blamed for faults in the equipment and little men in blue
coats appeared on the lineside carrying radar guns to set up
speed traps. The morning they arrived at Uffington when I was
on duty I realised at once what was about to happen and got
word to Didcot and Swindon, warning drivers of the speed
trap. Forewarned is forearmed and I was amused to see each
train coming by dead on regulation speed (or slower) with a
broad grin on the face of the driver while he blew on his horn
what was known colloquially as 'arseholes' to the officials on
the ground. Radar guns were a sneaky way of attacking a very
serious problem, they did not cure anything, they merely gave
officialdom a chance to haul a driver over the coals.

What was needed were hot axle-box detectors between
Didcot and Uffington and signals that could be placed to
'Danger' whenever required. Jim, Elwyn and I knew this and
we variously raised the matter with those in charge of us or the
signalling. The Area Manager's reaction was 'Well, it works
all right in France' while the Signal & Telegraph Department
stuck to its old chestnut that such provisions would be 'too
expensive' — as if a collision between an express train and a
derailed goods would be cheaper! There was a general feeling

of dissatisfaction among the Uffington and Reading signalmen at the *de haut en bas* attitude the Managers and the Technocrats adopted towards us; we were merely steam-age men grumbling about progress. Ted Blackall, in Reading Panel, promised that when he was called to the Ministry of Transport Inquiry into the Steventon job he would hammer home the signalman's objections to the system as it stood but there was no knowing when the Report would be published so Jim, Elwyn and I decided to do something drastic at once.

We invited our Member of Parliament and a reporter from the *Daily Mirror* to come to the signal box to see for themselves what we were complaining about and judge whether we were talking nonsense or not. At about 3 p.m. one day in early February all three of us, including Elwyn who was on night shift, were in the box waiting for our guests to arrive. The reporter from the *Daily Mirror* arrived first; we explained our case to him and at the end of the exposition he went off well pleased at being able to telephone his 'shock — horror' story to his editor in London. Shortly afterwards our MP arrived. Again we explained the position but his reaction was quite different. He granted that he could see why we were worried but felt that it would only alarm the public for the story to be published.

'Well, it's too late to keep it quiet now,' I said, 'a reporter from the *Daily Mirror* has gone off into the village to phone it back to his paper.'

'Don't worry about that,' he replied. 'Stories are always being ditched. You wouldn't want this made public.' Our MP went away leaving three very disappointed signalmen behind. We all insisted that we did but he was adamant and — for whatever reason — the report was not printed. We would have been much happier if he had told us that he would take our complaint to Western Region Management, for that is what he did, without saying anything to us. The meeting was arranged for 1 March at Paddington and duly took place. In reply to the criticisms he made of the signalling system he was told that arrangements were in hand to provide controlled signals every three miles and also hot axle-box detectors. The first part of that was an over-optimistic 'terminological inexactitude', the second part turned out to be correct.

The Ministry of Transport Inquiry into the Steventon derailment was conducted in public by Colonel McNaughton, RE, and was attended by journalists from several national newspapers and the BBC — such was the interest in the case, or rather series of cases. The newshounds were confounded by the dense railway jargon and the undoubted playing down of the dangerous aspects of the signalling system. However, having kept the questions and answers well under control the Colonel permitted himself the following observation in his Official report on the incident:

A disquieting feature of this accident was the disclosure by the signalman (Ted Blackall) that he was unable to stop oncoming traffic because none of the seven signals on the up line between Uffington and Steventon was provided with any means of replacing it to 'Danger' from the Panel.

Nine months after our MP's meeting at Paddington, Western Region installed emergency replacement switches in Reading Panel and Uffington signal box together with hot axle-box detectors at Wantage Road on the up and down main lines. Our detector was sited on the down line. Heat-sensing elements were placed outside each rail in order to check the left- and right-hand bearing of each axle. When a down train approached the sensors the recording instrument in Uffington box was automatically switched on. A roll of paper began to turn and two needles — representing the left- and right-hand ends of each axle — deflected as the axles passed the sensor. The needles traced black, parallel lines with each axle-box shown as a little, V-shaped blip. The type of train could be recognised from the tracing. Milk tanks with three axles produced a series of triple blips connected by a short, straight line; a passenger train gave two double blips, a long straight line and two more double blips as the close-coupled bogies passed and a goods train produced a serrated-edge effect as dozens of axles passed at 10-ft intervals. As the needles scratched busily from side to side they made the sound, familiar and much beloved, of wheels over rail joints to the rhythm of that type of train. I took an immediate liking to that machine — it had a 'human' aspect whilst making the safety of the line more certain.

When an overheated axle bearing passed a sensor an alarm buzzer sounded and an extra large blip — in proportion to the amount of overheating — showed precisely which axle in the train was at fault. The Uffington signalman could then turn the signal at Challow to 'Danger' to stop the train and could, if necessary, turn the up line signal to 'Danger' at Challow as well so that a train would not pass the defective train until the latter had come to a stand. This was in line with Regulation 17 of the signalling rules which we had been forced to ignore — with Western Region's tacit approval — since 1 June 1965. So, at long last, and after eighteen months of too many close encounters, the yokel signalmen of Uffington triumphed over haughty authority.

CHAPTER FIVE

BATTLE HARDENED

Just before Uffington signal box fell before the advance of Multiple Aspect Signalling, I had a job 'on the ground' at Challow, working the emergency cross-overs with Jim Spinage. There was to be an Engineers' occupation of the down main line between Challow and Uffington and so the up line would be converted, temporarily, to single-line working. I drove Jim down to the station from Childrey and we arrived at the ground frame, at the foot of the derelict platform ramp, just before 10 p.m. Darkness hid the worst of the decaying station and, indeed, we felt cheerful. There were lights on in the windows of the station cottages, strings of multi-coloured fairy-lights gleamed around the Prince of Wales pub and we were 'fresh on'. It was always pleasant for signalmen who normally saw each other only for a few minutes at change of shift (even though they lived in the same village) to work a whole shift together. A friendly, London Division Inspector joined us, having driven down from Reading in his yellow railway van and at 10 p.m. Elwyn, at Uffington, pressed the plunger to electrically unlock the key of the ground frame. One of us turned the big, brass Annett's key out of its lock and thereby switched to 'Danger' the signals on each side of the cross-over points whilst allowing the ground-frame levers to be pulled to switch the points when required. Until the key was restored those points were Jim's and my responsibility. Trains passed the up or down direction signal at 'Danger' on the instructions of the Pilotman. He was the guarantor of safety on the single-track section. He either ordered a driver to pass through the single line whilst remaining on the ground or he travelled through the section on the locomotive. Nothing moved over the single line without the Pilotman personally ordering the movement, face to face, with the driver so, theoretically, there could be no head-on collisions. Ensuring that the Pilotman was always at the right end of the single line required planning and teamwork, alertness after many hours out in the weather — and in bad weather the job became very tiring indeed. No one complained, each simply rose to the occasion.

An old hut which had once stood on the up side of the line for the use of a fogman had been carried across to the down side but for some unknown reason it had been parked on the sloping ramp of the platform instead of on level ground. Its brazier had come, too, so, gathering up lumps of splintered sleepers and even bits of coal fallen from the tenders of long-departed shunting engines, we lit a fire and set out on the night's work. Our job was to set the points either for a crossing movement from down main to up main or for the direct run, straight up the main when a train was coming from Uffington. When the points were reversed for a crossing movement they were held securely by clamping the switch rail to the stock rail with a massive, cast-iron clamp which was then padlocked until the points had again to be altered. This procedure also guarded against any alteration of the points through some momentary forgetfulness. Whichever way the points were set, one of us would stand by with a green hand-signal when everything was in order for a train to pass. A very important detail to note was to check that the Pilotman was on the passing train; he would shout out as he went by so that we knew that the next train would be coming from the opposite end of the line and therefore the points would have to be reversed. We were unprotected by any interlocking — we were manning a mid-Victorian-style operation and safety depended entirely on our alertness.

In the dark, long after the upstairs lights in the cottages had gone out and the last of the cars had roared tipsily out of the pub car park, Jim and I trudged the ballast with our lamps and point clamps, phoning, keeping up with the situation, setting the road, hand-signalling the trains as the dim silhouette of wheels rang through the night, squealing their flanges over the curving cross-overs, grinding their brakes as they stopped to drop the Pilot. Around 4 a.m. the last train for ninety minutes had gone, the next would be the 'York' and the 'Up Waker'. We were all feeling windblown and weary so the Pilotman and the Inspector went off for a kip in the yellow van while Jim and I fitted ourselves into the leaning 'foggin' 'ut'. It had been built to shelter one man in relative comfort and Jim, if he will forgive my saying so, was equivalent to 1½ — and we were both bulky in our railway-issue greatcoats. To fit in at all we sat with our arms around each other's shoulders like Tweedle-dum and Tweedledee. The fire burnt low and smoke began to sting our wind-scorched faces so we pulled the door to and slept on a plank seat.

I woke on all fours on the cinders beside the track, wondering where the hell I was. Behind me was the sound of struggle and, getting up and turning round, I saw the grey shape of the hut, lying on its side and Jim crawling out through the fallen-open door. In sleep I must have leaned on him; he must have leaned on the hut; and, with the assistance of an extra-strong gust of wind, it had overbalanced. The sky was greying with dawn. I had the taste of thermos flask tea and sandwiches, stale in my mouth, my joints were stiff with cold.

'Wassa-time, Jim?' I croaked.

He peered at his watch. 'Nearly time for the "York". You go and get them two out of the van, I'll phone Elwyn and see where it is.'

The railway came to life. The 'York' went down with the Pilotman and the 'Up Waker' — the 5.45 p.m. Penzance to Paddington sleeping-car train — came up, bringing with it blessed 'going home time', hence its nickname. Work was fun but it was also fun when it stopped. I had worked my last shift at Challow and, shortly afterwards, on 3 March 1968, I worked my last at Uffington when the box was closed under the Swindon MAS scheme.

Jim and Elwyn left the railway at this juncture but, like Deputy Dawg in the TV cartoon series of the time, I wanted to see what would happen next. I had had fifty years' ration of emergencies, failures and assorted crises in my three years at Uffington. I felt 'battle hardened', and confident of my ability to cope with whatever might befall. I took a vacancy at Kennington Junction, 2¾ miles south of Oxford station. The box was an 18-mile drive from Childrey, so I sold my Morris 8 and bought a Jowett 'Javelin' for the daily journey. The signal box was curiously difficult to find on the first visit. Through gaps between the houses lining the main road I caught glimpses of its roof but, driving up and down, could find no way in until I realised that what I had taken to be a gap in a hedge was the entrance to a very narrow, stony lane leading to the railway line between tall, overgrown hedges. At the bottom was a five-bar gate protecting the tracks. It was truly a 'down the rabbit-hole' situation; once through this dark passage the manic rush of the tarmac road was left behind and instead the world was rural, peaceful and orderly.

The signal box was tall and dignified, built in 1901 of smooth, red brick with blue corner bricks and a handsome brick chimney rising above a hip-gabled roof. It stood on the up side of the line, its back to the main line, facing the branch. I learned the job — and there was a great deal to learn — with Don Symonds. From the tall signal box we looked out on an interesting layout. Four tracks ran northwards to Hinksey South box and Oxford station, double track curved away southwards to Radley and Didcot while the single-track branch line to Morris Cowley climbed steeply and curved eastwards over the river Thames. Northwards the trains were semaphore signalled on goods and passenger lines; southwards they ran under automatic, colour-light signals and to Cowley they ran under traditional signals with the electric train token to ensure safety on the single line. We worked with Reading Panel so there was a train describer on the instrument shelf but this one seemed quite a civilised machine and gave little trouble. Although the colour-lights as little as a mile away were part of Reading Panel's empire the three ground frames between Kennington and Radley, 2½ miles away, were

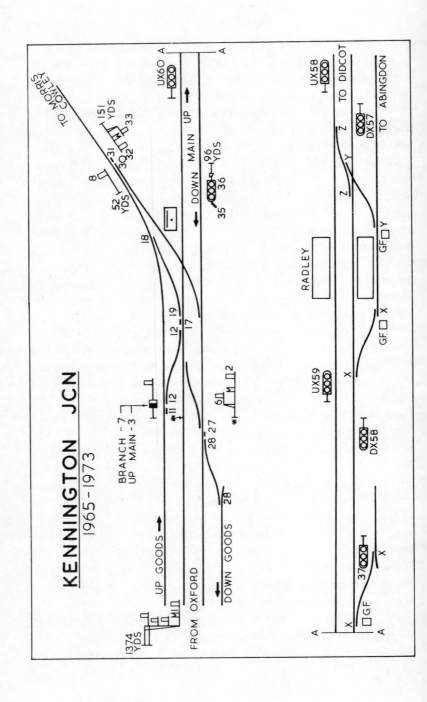

KENNINGTON JCN
1965 - 1973

controlled from Kennington and were in daily use, giving access to the Abingdon branch and the refrigerated meat store at Sandford.

The branch line climbed at 1 in 93 to cross the Thames on a fine 'bow and string' steel-girder bridge dating from 1923. On the far side of the branch tracks, opposite the signal box, was a mysterious area of swamp, forested by willows of great age, their corded trunks forked and twisted, their branches long, drooping and riotously entangled. To the left of the view a hawthorn hedge rose raggedly all but hiding a ruined boat-house, landlocked then but obviously built when the river lapped the foot of the railway embankment. In front of the hedge was the brick lower portion of the original (1870) Kennington Junction box used since 1901 by the Permanent Way Department as a store shed. Along the branch, 250 yards to the right, past a tall bracket signal with two posts and three arms, the handsome old bridge finally penned off the area of tussocky swamp. Any slight breeze turned the spearblade-shaped leaves of the willows. In spring, when the sun was bright and keen, they danced and flickered green and silver but at night when the moon was bright they hung motionless, the colour of mercury against the deep shadows inside the forest while the gnarled trunks, catching the light, turned a ghostly silver. In autumn, when the mist rose off the river, the trees were hidden until the sun broke through and they emerged slowly out of a champagne-coloured haze; in winter the same mist rose from the water and froze fantastically on every twig.

Just south of the signal box, down between the converging embankments of the two routes, there was a large mobile home where two good-looking teenage girls lived with their parents. To see them in their garden or to have them visit the signal box was an unusual and very pleasant addition to life at Kennington. It was useful, too, because when they went shopping they would come up and ask if they could get anything in the food line for me. They were friendly and direct, as if they had always known me and I never asked them their names. After the mud and chaos of Uffington, Kennington seemed like Nirvana, a haven of sanity and peace in what had been a very naughty world.

Although the box was working with Reading Panel and although I handled about seventy-five trains a shift — half as much again as at Uffington — they went by without memorable fuss. The working was more intricate than at Uffington, it worked well and I was able to enjoy the job. Only once do I recall the old nightmare impinging on my riverside idyll. About noon one day I received 6 bells from the Panel; I acknowledged it and went onto the telephone to be told the reason for sending the code. A Swansea express had been standing at the up platform at Didcot, waiting for a down express from Paddington to Worcester to go across the four main lines to the Didcot avoiding line, as it were, 'across the bows' of the Swansea although at a distance of perhaps 300 yards. As the down Worcester reached the junction facing points in the down main, travelling at 40 mph or a little less, the 'switch diamonds' in the up main line had suddenly reversed for normal, 'straight-up-the-main' running. The Worcester train was therefore diverted down the up main line but came to a stand without colliding with the Swansea. That was the nearest I got to 'shock-horror' at Kennington, which was perfectly acceptable to me.

Pinned on the wall of the box was a yellowing newspaper cutting concerning an instance of real 'shock-horror' straight out of an Alfred Hitchcock film. Down the branch line a mile or so was Littlemore mental hospital and one night an inmate walked into Kennington box to demand that the signalman, Pete Hall, stop a train to take him to London. Pete knew he was an inmate because he was wearing nothing but a vest of immodestly short length and was carrying a large, pointed, kitchen knife. Pete kept calm and was able to talk the man out of his plan — he was hardly dressed for travelling, after all — and was then able to telephone for assistance. Whilst glad not to have been placed in such a situation, at the same time I felt a slight wave of envy when I read the cutting; I would have liked to have known how I would have coped.

My relief at Kennington was an old-hand railwayman, Jack Gough, who had been on duty in Appleford Crossing box on the night of 13 November 1942 when 2975 *Lord Palmer*, with seventy-two wagons weighing 770 tons, was driven off the end of the down goods loop just as 4088 *Dartmouth Castle*, with eleven coaches, was passing down the main line. I had known Jack since my visits to Didcot East Junction in the early 1960s; he was of the species 'slow but sure'. When Jack told me about the crash he said that, before accepting any train on the down goods loop from Didcot North box, he always checked first to see that the stop signal lamp at his end of the loop was burning. I had never before heard of this excellent precaution being taken; I was impressed and, knowing Jack of old, I was quite prepared to believe he did that — every time. On each shift at Kennington he came through the gateway ten or fifteen minutes before time, wheeling his bike carefully and shutting the gate with an air of intense concentration that was his hallmark. Never mind that I would want to drive through that gate in ten minutes, that gate had to be kept shut to prevent anything running down the lane and onto the line — so shut it was.

Regarding the Appleford crash, the down loop line ended 70 yards short of his signal box, directly in line with it. Jack said he had the signals 'off' for the express and was looking out for it. 'I could see the headlights of a train coming towards me,' he told me, 'and I thought it was the fast, judging by the rate they were coming yet the lamps seemed too close together to be "A" headcode and I opened the window to see better — you know how signal-box window glass is so wavy it can distort things. Well, as soon as I did that I could see it was the goods and I could see it wasn't going to stop at the board.' Jack spoke slowly and quietly, just like his actions. He said he went straightaway and put his down line signals to 'Danger' and sent 'Obstruction Danger' even before the accident happened — but even then, I don't suppose he rushed! As a matter of interest, 4088 got past before the goods was derailed but the rear six coaches were badly smashed up and two people were killed. 2975 overturned at about 25 mph, killing the driver,

Mr Furse of Newport (Mon.), and his fireman, R.A. Jarvis of Didcot.

Don Symonds, Jack and I worked round the three shifts, twenty days consecutively before getting one day, a Sunday, free which might or might not have been taken up with hand-signalman's duties on some engineering task. Changing shifts at weekends was particularly wearisome. After working from 10 p.m. to 6 a.m. every day until Sunday morning, back again on Sunday evening at 6 p.m. until 6 a.m. Monday morning and then back again at 2 p.m. that same day for another week of eight-hour shifts. The hours became more difficult as one drew towards the end of a week and one became more tired but at least Don and I had the internal combustion engine to carry us to and from work. Jack Gough, at the age of about sixty-three, cycled 7½ miles each way no matter what the weather, no matter how short the time before he had to be back at work yet I do not recall him ever being late in the signal box.

On the Cowley line there was an intermediate siding at what had been Littlemore station for the benefit of a Shell oil and petroleum depot. The points leading into the siding were operated by the guard of the train, who released the lock on the lever with the key on the end of the electric train token. The train for this siding ran on most days and was belled from Hinksey North to Kennington as a '1–2' accompanied by the cryptic telephone message: 'That's a little more oil'. The token system came to the Great Western in 1914 and was utterly reliable. Once one aluminium token had been taken from the bright red, cast-iron instrument, no other token could be withdrawn either from the Kennington or the Morris Cowley instrument until the first token had been restored to the instrument and no train driver would enter on the single track unless he had possession of a token. After the token was removed from the electric lock of the instrument it was clipped into a steel, hooped carrier and taken outside to be placed on the lineside standard from which it would be snatched by one of the engine crew. Trains returning from Cowley passed very close to the north corner of the signal box so the token in its carrier was always handed up to the signalman leaning out of the window rather than the driver dropping it onto the 'cow's horn' provided for the purpose a few yards away from the box. The walk along the ballast to set the carrier on the post and the shouted greetings as we swapped the token off a train from Cowley gave me great satisfaction and a sense of enjoyment, the feeling of being a vital part of the railway and its time-honoured rituals.

The branch rose steeply from Kennington all the way to Wheatley tunnel, 4½ miles away, at gradients varying between 1 in 77 and 1 in 93. The top end of the incline was known as 'Horspath bank' and in steam days had been considered a formidable obstacle. At Oxford station one day, long ago, the guard of a train going to London via Wheatley and Princes Risborough informed the driver of his load and added that some of the weight was made up of four horse-boxes at the rear of the train. At that the driver 'reared-up', to use a local term, and stated emphatically that his engine would not be able to get up Horspath 'wi' that lot taked on the back'. The guard muttered, 'Oh, all right,' and went away and after a few minutes gave the signal and the train left. Above Horspath Halt the train ground to a stand, the guard got down and walked forward to see what was the matter and was greeted by the driver: 'There you are, what did I tell you?' said he. 'I knew we wouldn't get up "Horspath" with that lot on.' The guard was astonished: 'But we haven't got them on — after what you said I had them taken off.' Then it was the driver's turn to be astonished and the train started away on the steep gradient and sailed over the summit without any fuss.

On rare occasions the steep gradient overpowered the engine's brakes on the downhill journey, this being in the days of unbraked trains when only the engine and the guard's van had a brake. About 1957 a 'Hall' class engine was standing at the Kennington end of Morris Cowley station, waiting for a goods train to arrive from the Wheatley direction, the intention being to stop the latter train and then let each train carefully into the passing loops. The goods from Wheatley was hauled by an ex-LMS 2–8–0. The driver was braking the engine but the weight of the train running forward onto the engine drove it on in a wheels-locked skid. The driver took the brake off and re-applied it but the train was out of control, ran through the station and crashed into the 'Hall' waiting on the single track at the far end of the layout. The driver of the 'Hall' was taken by surprise so his engine was standing with its brakes hard on against the gradient when the 2–8–0 struck home. Their boilers were smashed and the 'Hall's' frames, made of inch-thick steel, were bent back like tinfoil.

Stopping an unbraked train was hazardous because the weight of the train was usually so much greater than that of the engine but in June 1965 a train of 'car flats', each fitted with a vacuum brake under the driver's control, ran away approaching Kennington Junction from Cowley and was derailed across the main line, scattering new cars onto the tracks.

The most difficult job I had at Kennington was working the Abingdon branch trip to Radley and getting it onto the branch without stopping passenger trains. The Abingdon ran from Oxford South End or Hinksey yards between 6 and 6.30 a.m. behind a couple of trips to Cowley and another for Littlemore. They came along the up goods line from Hinksey South and queued nose to tail waiting their turn down the single-track branch. There were also five trains scheduled on the up main line between 6 and 6.50 a.m.; two 90 mph 'Freightliners', an ordinary goods and two passenger trains, the second of these leaving Oxford at 6.46 a.m. By that time the Cowley train had gone leaving the Abingdon standing first in the loop ready to follow the 6.46 a.m. Oxford up the main line. From then until 7.25 a.m. there was a gap in the up line traffic but on the down line the 2.10 a.m. Cardiff to Corby coal was due to pass Didcot North at 7 a.m. followed by the first down passenger train, due to call at Radley at 7.15 a.m. I had fifteen minutes or so to get the Abingdon onto its branch. With luck it would be D63xx or even 'Hymek' hauled so that the 2½ miles to Radley could be covered in about six minutes but very often there was only what I was pleased to call a 'mechanical tortoise' — a grimy, grinding, diesel shunter with a top speed of 15 mph. There was practically no other time of day to run the Abingdon, it had to go out behind the 6.46 Oxford and any late-running 'Freight-liner' coming up behind the passenger just had to wait its turn behind the branch trip.

The train usually consisted of twenty 'car flats' as well as any traffic in coal or for the meat store so it was around 460 yards long. At Radley the train stopped to let the guard off at the ground frame and then drew its quarter-mile-long tail clear of the points. If the train was shunter-hauled the Cardiff coal train would by now be clicking into my describer. The guard phoned to ask for the key, I pressed the plunger. If the guard was expert he would flick the key out of its lock in a second, if he was not . . . The Annett's key liked to be treated nicely, it had to be turned with a certain rolling action or else the lock would jam. Patiently pressing the plunger and watching the clock, I visualised the progress over the ground of the coal train. When the key for the ground frame was removed it set the signal protecting the points on the up and down line to 'Danger' and obviously this had to happen at such a time that the driver of the oncoming train was given a proper 'Caution' signal. It was no good flicking a green signal to red in the face of 750 tons moving at 40 mph. If the guard was ham-fisted or if for some other reason time was getting short, I had to stop him and let the coal train pass then the down passenger train would be close behind so the branch train had to wait for that as well and was therefore blocking the up line as the time for the 7.25 a.m. Oxford drew close. Working the Abingdon was quite a game. Later in the morning the return trip had to be worked from Radley to Sandford, reverse into the siding and then out again for the 'dash', if that is the right word for a diesel shunter's progress, to the goods loop at Kennington. The line fell from Sandford and with the assistance of gravity unusually high speed was possible. I went out on the shunter hauling the Abingdon trip one morning and drove it back from Abingdon. It was automatically governed to 15 mph and its speedometer was not calibrated past 20 mph but, once the train was clear of the points at Sandford, I gave the wretched little machine full throttle and in no time at all the speedometer needle was hard against the stop. We might have been running at 25 mph!

After nine months at Kennington a vacancy arose at a much bigger and more challenging box: Hinksey North. It was in a higher grade of pay than Kennington but because it was switched-out from noon each Saturday until Monday morning there was less money to be earned there than at Kennington. Quite apart from having more trains to work with at Hinksey North I would have every weekend free to go as a volunteer fireman on the Festiniog Railway. I applied for the job and as no one else wanted less pay for more work I got the job — arguably the busiest manual signal box in the London Division. I passed the usual rules examination and took the job on with a special piece of advice from the Oxford District Inspector ringing in my ears: 'Keep a sharp look-out on the track and on that bridge over the Thames when the Schools* are coming up. Some of the students get suicidal tendencies around then.'

* University examination time.

CHAPTER SIX

SHIFTS WITH SHUNTERS

To save a long drive twice a day — or night — I looked for lodgings in Oxford. I had great difficulty in knowing where to start. The streets nearest the box were decidedly intimidating to a first-time lodging-seeker so in the end I started knocking on doors in north Oxford, an area much beloved by John Betjeman, full of stately, Victorian houses which were in turn full of University students. After a lot of traipsing up and down the streets and front garden paths I discovered a room to let in a house owned by a very jolly lady who worked on cancer research at the Churchill Hospital. Her small son David had a train set and I think she had some idea that I would play with it and him and thus keep him amused when I was not at work.

My new-found lodgings were about 2½ miles from Hinksey North, a pleasant cycle ride either along Walton Street's rows of little shops and great buildings such as the Oxford University Press and Worcester College, or down Woodstock Road and through tree-lined St Giles, turning down between the Randolph Hotel and the Ashmolean Museum at the Martyrs' Memorial. Access to the signal box was through the gates of the South End yard, opposite the rear entrance of the GPO sorting office, alongside a sort of 'Peabody Building' tenement of seedy and secretive aspect where there was not a 'Dreaming Spire' or an American blue-rinse to be seen. One evening I saw parked outside this 'Peabody Building,' a customised Morris Mini-Minor, all chromium plate, rows of headlamps, ultra-wide wheels and a hydra-headed exhaust pipe, also beautifully chromed. Coming out through the gates next morning I saw the same car standing on bricks, chrome strip and headlamps missing, wheel-less, the ends of the stubby axles like little fists appealing for justice.

The signal box stood about 80 yards south of a bridge over the Thames, on the down side of the line about half a mile south of Oxford station. It was very plain to look at. Built in 1941 to withstand bomb-blasts and bomb-splinters, it was a brick block house with a flat, concrete roof — the GWR version of the standard 'ARP' (Air Raid Precautions) signal box. The man who taught me the job, Stan Worsfold, had spent his life working Oxford's signal boxes. He told me that Hinksey North had been built by Italian prisoners of war who came flocking to work each day, on their bikes, from a camp on Cumnor Hill, singing their heads off and their military escort being not very much in evidence. The Italians' knowledge of bricklaying was minimal but with good supervision from McAlpine's foremen they did a good job although the sudden lapse from English Bond to Italian confusion in the right-hand back corner of the box suggested that a foreman had taken a day off on one occasion. The signal box was brought into use in April 1942 and took the place of the old Oxford South box in controlling the South End yard on the north side of the river on the up side of the line and, in addition, worked the north end of the new 'Hinksey' yard, south of the river on the down side. Stan Worsfold had been signalman in the old South box and had carried the train register across the bridge to start work again in the new Hinksey North box, three times the size of his old workplace.

The new yard had been laid across low-lying ground intersected with streams and in exploring my newly acquired and far-flung empire I discovered part of an inscription made by an Italian in the then wet cement of a culvert he was helping to build. Some of the finger-drawn letters had been lost as the surface flaked away but it was clear that the man had recorded his name, the name of his regiment and, in big letters, the English words 'Master Mason'. This was on the largest of the culverts and he had obviously been very pleased with it.

From the front window of the box I looked over the ruin that had once been Oxford's gas works to the 'Dreaming Spires' of the University. Merton Tower I could see, St Mary's in the High, All Souls, the dome of the Sheldonian and, close enough to be able to read the time on its clock face, the octagonal 'Tom Tower' of Christchurch whose bells marked off the passing hours of my shifts. In the still of the night, Oxford seems to be a city of clocks. Just beyond the fence the old gas works was a ragwort and grassy wilderness of piled bricks, bent pipes and rusting steel, colonised by rabbits that were preyed upon by feral cats. In wet weather the 'Dreaming Spires' vanished behind grey rain and the desolation of the scene was grim indeed but on bright, sunny days, the rusty, flower-strewn ground had a strangely pretty look.

From the towpath along the Thames, a footpath came up the embankment to rail level at the rear of the signal box. One very wet, cold day, I was looking south watching for an approaching train, when I noticed what looked like a pile of sacks lying near the down main line. I thought something had fallen from a train, looked again this time through the open window and saw that the 'sacks' was a person, on all fours, the head pressed against the ground, the arms around the head. With the down train 'getting handy' I hurried downstairs, ran to the person and, rather nervously, touched the shoulder. The body gave a nervous start and the head raised. It was a girl, about twenty years old, obviously very distressed. I squatted down and asked her to come into the box but she made no move; the rain was pelting down and the train was imminent so I pulled her gently to her feet and led her inside. She walked in a leaden, automatic way. Her outer clothing was soaked and, indeed, she was probably soaked to the skin but I could hardly suggest that she take off her clothes. The fire was hot in the big, iron stove so I drew the armchair close and into its threadbare and somewhat grimy embrace she crept, curled up and slept. I put my coat over her and throughout three hours of clangorous bells and thumping levers she lay as if dead and there were times when I forgot she was there. Around 1 p.m. she woke and got stiffly to her feet, my overcoat around her shoulders, her hair all damp and bedraggled. She refused my offer of food and hot drinks and when I asked, 'Isn't there anything I can do to help?' the first recognisable expression passed over her face, not actually a smile but at least a lightening of that dreadful 'dead' look. She also spoke the first and last words she uttered to me: 'You've been a great help.' With that she put my coat down on the chair and hurried out of the box, turning down the footpath to the river. An awful thought struck me. I telephoned the shunters' cabin, explained the situation rapidly and asked that one of them go onto the bridge, watch the girl and make sure she saw him watching. Moments later I saw Cyril Main hurrying across the tracks to lean over the steel parapet. A few seconds later he walked back to the hut and telephoned to say that everything was all right. The girl had walked along the path towards Osney leaving nothing but speculation behind her.

The shunters on my shift were a team of three and some-times four. The foreman and Cyril had spent a lifetime on the railway at Oxford, following in the footsteps of fathers and grandfathers. Another man was a cheerful, heavyweight Pole called Marion. On night-shift their work was particularly tiring as the train service called them out to strenuous work in any weather when the rest of Oxford and most of their fellow railwaymen were asleep — or at any rate taking a brief nap. And when the shunters were at work so was the signalman in Hinksey North — another reason why, top class box though it was, it had only one regular signalman: me. It was, in the phrase of the time, 'never paid for'. There were only forty-three to forty-five trains on night-shift but of those nine or ten called to work in Hinksey or South End yards, so while other signalmen might have their feet up, the man in Hinksey North was busy with the shunters, switching the points in response to the telephoned commands, 'Shed side' or 'Field side up', working a trip across to Hinksey yard or sending an engine from the South End to the diesel depot 'wrong road' on the up goods loop.

The 11.40 p.m. Paddington to Worcester goods stopped on the down main line to detach traffic for Oxford and went on its way leaving the yard pilot to come out onto the main line to collect the wagons and take them back to the yard in a shunt of entertaining complication. Trains of empty 'car flats' arrived from Johnstone in Scotland and from Parkstone Quay, Essex, to terminate in one or other of the yards; trains of petrol from Fawley refinery; trains of empties going back to the refinery; trains of general merchandise — all this traffic called, shunted and moved on. The diesel shunter pilot engine hauled out rakes of wagons, freshly loaded from the goods shed and placed empty wagons for loading; newly arrived traffic had to be berthed for unloading; trains were formed at night for morning trips to Charlbury, Bicester, Cowley, Littlemore and Abingdon. The hard-pressed shunters spent most of the night walking or running between rows of wagons, coupling and uncoupling with their long, hickory poles, waving on, calling back and stopping movements with their hand-lamp signal (unless there was a fog when the work became a near impossibility), sorting wagons while the next train waited its turn on the up loop or down reception line.

One night a train of petrol was on the down reception line in Hinksey yard, waiting its turn in the South End. After an hour the door of the signal box was flung open and heavy boots came stamping up the stairs.

'If I have to wait another five minutes I'll cut off and go home!' snarled the very fed-up driver of the Class 33 diesel on the petrol train, its distinctive 'tonking' tick-over coming faintly down the track and through the open door.

'You won't go anywhere unless I pull off for you,' I snapped back. 'You can see for yourself that they're hard at it in South End. They'll take you when they're ready.'

'They ought to stop and let us over then, I could drop my stuff and go.'

'There's nowhere for you to put it, is there, that's what they're working on. Tell you what,' I continued in a consoling tone, 'you ought to have a "King Arthur" down there instead of that bloody old diesel with you on it all by yourself. Then you and your mate could make some tea on the shovel in the fire and get the cards out on the bucket.'

The driver brightened at once. 'Aha! Now you're talking!'

'Well, OK then,' I said, 'you put the kettle on for us now and we'll have one together.' I was sorry when the shunters asked 'Let's have the Fawley over'; the driver and I were having a great old gas about Southern steam!

I relished working Hinksy North because it allowed me to feel more like a signalman than ever. We were permitted such complications as working in the wrong direction over the up goods loop — the 'Old Main' — between South End and the station — bell code 2.3.3; we could use the 'Warning Acceptance', 3.5.5, and the 'Line Clear to Clearing Point Only', 2.2.2, as well. We were also allowed to give 'Train out of Section' for an up train while that train was still inside the clearing point providing that it was proceeding on its journey, this last to save a few vital seconds and help keep traffic running through the bottleneck that was Oxford station. Doubtless this attitude was naive and over-enthusiastic but that is how I felt. I think it was my over-eager disposition that annoyed the foreman shunter; any enthusiasm he might have had for trains had long since been washed out in the gales and snows of forty winters in the yard. Anyhow, he took a dislike to me which made life difficult at times.

One dark and moonless night he phoned and gruffly ordered the road, 'Shed side to Hinksey Down yard,' slamming his phone down before I had a chance to reply. He was going to take the returned empty 'car flats' from Johnstone over into Hinksey yard, the engine which had brought them from the north having gone to shed 'wrong road' over the up loop. I set the road and over went twenty 'car flats' behind a diesel shunter. I watched carefully to see the red tail-light disappear and reappear three times and then reversed the levers for normal, up and down, running. Stan Worsfold had shown me this trick of knowing, in the dark, when the last vehicle of a train was clear of points 200 yards away. There was a line of electricity supply poles down in the yard and when the tail-lamp had come out from behind the third one the train was clear of the points.

Half an hour later a train of 'car flats' from Bathgate was

belled up the main. These were destined for Cowley so they could go onto the up reception line between me and Hinksey South box. Number 2 up loop was already blocked and No 1 up loop was required for through trains. I told Johnny Blanchard at Hinksey South what was happening, set the points and lowered the signals. As the train turned into the up reception line a horrid thought occurred to me. The shunters were still in Hinksey down yard with their pilot engine and had been there for some time. There was a connection* from the down reception to the up reception line which was operated by the shunters *after* they had asked the signalman at Hinksey North if it was safe to do so. The traffic-worn foreman was unlikely to ask a young sprig like me for permission to move about 'his' yard. I went to the window, slid it back and listened. Sure enough, a few seconds later there came that nasty, sullen, thump that speaks of collisions. The signal protecting the connection had been at 'Danger' (this also was worked by the shunters) but its light was out and the driver had not seen it until too late so his engine cut through the middle of the Johnstone 'car flats' as they stood across the connection. The foreman used the ground frame telephone then gave me a colourful description of what he was going to do to me when he got back to the signal box. He never came and it was, as my Granny used to say, 'Sam-Fairy-Ann' to me; he had dropped the clanger and he would have to carry the can. I do not recall that anyone in charge made any inquiry into the incident. If the damage was not too severe it was likely that the 'family' atmosphere of the railway kept it covered up.

Three weeks later I was again on night-shift when the lamp in No 1 up goods loop starting signal went out. It was one of three on a gantry over the main line and it was most important that it be re-lit, to comply with Rule 74. The shunters were hard at work and if I went to light the lamp all their work would stop. It seemed that the best plan would be for one of them to go and light it. I rang their telephone long and loud till the dreaded foreman answered.

* See X, Y, Z on diagram on p. 88.

'What do you want?' he snapped.

'Could one of you come and light the lamp in the up loop starter, please?'

'I've told you before — you do your job and I'll do mine.' Slam. Down went his phone.

'All right,' I said into the dead mouthpiece, 'I will.' I looked for some paraffin, found none and realised I would have to get some from the shunters' store. This was going to be a longer job than I thought; up to the shunters' cabin, probably have a row with the foreman, then back past the box to the gantry to fix the lamp. Rule 74 forbade me to leave the signal box for this purpose unless all my signals were at 'Danger'. There was going to be a certain amount of delay. I told the signalmen at the station and at Hinksey South what I was doing and left the box.

I walked down the track to the accompaniment of furious whistlings from the pilot. The shunters wanted the road out from 'Shed side'. I found three of them silhouetted in the light coming from the open door of their cabin, huddled together, their shunting poles resting on the ground like medieval pikes. They looked distinctly unhappy. Inside the hut the foreman was leaning with his shoulder against the ringing button of the telephone. 'Can I have some paraffin, please, Cyril?' I asked. My sudden appearance out of the darkness caused pandemonium.

The fireman came out of the hut at the gallop, braying, 'What the hell are you doing here? What are you playing at?' He was still raving as Cyril, who was a decent sort, hurried me away to the oil store. He had heard my earlier request and had volunteered to light the lamp but had been over-ruled. It took about half an hour to light that lamp and the shunters lost that much time from their bonus. Luckily there were very few trains running, or wanting to run, through Oxford at that time of night. Anyhow, after this the foreman was no longer hostile and we co-existed in a state of armed neutrality.

On eight-hour shifts I had time to visit other signal boxes, to photograph the railway or around the streets of Oxford. There was shopping to be done for the one large meal of the day, food to be prepared for the next day's work, the launderette to be visited, sometimes when it was full at ten in the morning, sometimes when it seemed weirdly empty, near midnight. Occasionally I had time to walk across Port Meadow in the twilight to the Trout at Godstow. On Saturdays I had the signal box switched out within seconds of the yard pilot clearing Oxford Station South box on its way to the diesel depot. The Jowett was parked outside the box and I would be away to Portmadoc for the Festiniog Railway. But on twelve-hour shifts there was little time for the background preparation necessary for the work itself — and I began to be asked to work more and more 'twelve hours'. I liked the work so I never thought of refusing and, indeed, I liked the overtime which could be saved and spent later on a full week as a fireman on the Festiniog Railway but those long shifts with very little chance to rest in the box, even on night-shift, became increasingly arduous. One great difficulty was shopping. On 'twelve-hour days' I did not get into the streets at the end of a shift until after 6 p.m., which left only one, wickedly expensive delicatessen from which to buy provisions — apart from Mrs Kennedy's butcher shop at the top of the Kingston Road. So, on the Saturday before a week of 6 a.m. to 6 p.m. shifts, I had to go to Marks & Spencer or Littlewoods and stock up with food, especially food for eating in the signal box — seven tins of Irish stew and seven tins of Wall's steak & kidney pie! At the end of a day I would cycle home along Walton Street, call at sympathetic Mrs Kennedy's shop for a big pork chop and some vegetables, then home to cook it all in the shared, basement, kitchen.

Opposite the kitchen door was the door of the bed-sit of a poor old lady who had rather been dumped there by her grown-up and very superior children. When she heard me rattling the pots and pans she came out to have, probably, the only conversation of her day. She was a little, thin old lady, anxious to impress upon me how unused she was to this kind of life. I was very sorry for her but found her pathetic and just a little scary so I always took my food upstairs to my room where, I, too, ate in solitude. Even quite nice food tastes flat when eaten without the sauce of some congenial company.

Going to work at 5.30 a.m. for ten to six in the box I had the streets to myself. The previous night's litter, from people eating on the hoof, blew aimlessly about the road or lay greasily in the gutters. There was only one person whom I was likely to see, only one person I wanted to see: Henry Wiggins, the milkman. Henry was eighty-three, though I would never have known if he had not proudly informed me of the fact. He was a short, stocky man with a trilby hat, a white moustache and a cheerful expression. He had been doing this round all his life and had used a horse and cart until the war when he had had to give up the horse. He then built himself the three-wheeled electric trolley, painted maroon, that I became familiar with. I could have bought a bottle of milk the day before but it was far better to buy it from Henry and have a few, friendly words in the darkness and rain of the early morning street or in the stillness of a summer dawn among those rather fine, early nineteenth-century houses at the city end of Walton Street.

'Doing for myself' at the end of long shifts, I began to fray at the edges. At first this 'fraying' had no effect on my work but off-duty forgetfulness was occasionally a nuisance. Cycling home at 2.30 p.m. I once pedalled right past the end of my road. I looked down it, saw that my bike was not leaning against the paving stones outside my lodging and was seized by a great wave of panic. Someone had stolen my bike! I leaped off my bicycle and only then realised that I was riding it and that I had gone by the end of my road. I must have been in a waking dream in the saddle.

I was in the world yet hardly a part of it for I seemed to be either in my room getting ready for work, at work, or cycling home from the signal box. I returned to my room one evening in late November at 6.30, thoroughly whacked after a twelve-hour shift. I threw my bag down and sat on the edge of the bed saying — and I clearly recall it even now — 'Phew! I'll just have a breather before I start the meal.' The next thing I knew I was waking from a deep sleep, stretched full length on the bed with a mouth that tasted like a sewer. I could not make out what had happened, groped for the switch of the bedside lamp, turned it on and saw the hands of the clock straight up and down. Six o'clock! I had slept all night and now I should be late for work. Without another moment's thought I dashed out of the house, onto my bike and pedalled madly away down Woodstock Road. I had no food or milk, all that mattered was to relieve my mate who had been at work all night.

As I hurried through the wide thoroughfare of St Giles it occurred to me that there was a lot of traffic about and lights on for 6 a.m. but I pedalled on, wondering how best to apologise to my colleague in the box. I cycled past the shunters, hard at work and hoped they would not notice I was late. Opposite the signal box I dismounted to carry the bike across the tracks and, looking up through the windows at the big, wooden cased clock to see how late I was, I saw the hands showing 11.45 p.m. I blinked and looked again, utterly at a loss. Then the penny dropped. I had not seen 6 a.m. on my clock but 11.30 p.m., the hands straight up and down. I crossed the tracks and slipped quietly away to the riverside path, out to Osney and home for five hours' sleep before another twelve-hour shift.

After this I resolved to say something to the rostering Inspector, Charlie Pavey. He phoned from Reading on Thursday to see if I was all right for twelve hours the following week.

'Couldn't you find an extra chap for here? A week of eight-hours would be like a holiday for me.'

'Get off — you like the overtime,' he replied, jollying me along.

'If I was to leave the job you'd have to find someone else,' I replied darkly.

Charlie laughed. 'Come on, you'd never leave — now then, what about this twelve hours next week?' I did not care to refuse — and not merely because of the near-double wages I should get. All my training throughout my life, including five years in the army as an adolescent, had been to obey whoever was in charge. But there was also a feeling now that I was being taken for granted which irked me. As it happened, I had recently been offered a whole winter as a fireman on the Festiniog Railway with lodgings in a lovely house overlooking Cardigan Bay. I agreed to the week of twelve hours but I also handed in my notice to terminate my service at the end of that week.

On 10 December 1969 I was in Boston Lodge shed on the Festiniog Railway, raising steam on *Blanche* as I polished her brass and paintwork.

CHAPTER SEVEN

LINESIDE POLICEMAN

The winter sojourn in Merioneth was a rugged but very pleasant interlude — I like the hills in winter when they are shrouded in drizzle and the lichens glisten on the great, grey boulders. However, mundane considerations such as the lack of folding money dictated a return to 'civilisation' and in March 1970 I was back in Oxford. I got lodgings in a little, bay-windowed house in Abbey Road, a dark, seedy-looking street close to the station and a very useful coffee shack. The Thames flowed level with the back yard and I suspect that the houses' foundations were sunk below the waterline in soggy clay. The inner end of the street, that furthest from the Botley Road, terminated at a wall bordering the canal beyond which was the engine shed — or what was left of it. Abbey Road houses crowded in on each other, shutting out the sun in an effort to sit on the narrow piece of level ground between the railway embankment and the river. The area had once housed a colony of railway families but by 1970 most railwaymen were rich enough to live in more salubrious parts of the City of Dreaming Spires.

My landlady was very cheerful and hard-working. She agreed not only to cook my meals but also to do my washing besides allowing me the use of her back room upstairs, overlooking the oily-green Thames, and all this for a very reasonable consideration. With these domestic arrangements confirmed by advance payments I went to the station and lurked nonchalantly and quite by chance right outside the District Inspector's door at just about the time he would normally emerge to carry the daily notices around the signal boxes. In about the time it took to whistle 'All you need is love' he appeared and, taking the apparition before him in his short, jaunty stride, said, 'Hello, Adrian, want your job back?' I was expecting a rather more protracted interview, a more searching inquisition so the surprise swept away any semblance of nonchalence and I gasped, 'Yes, please, where shall I go?'

'Hinksey North, of course. The job you left is still there. Here,' he said, handing me some beige, railway envelopes, 'take Stan Worsfold his Notices.'

Barely able to keep to a walk, I hurried down the path to the signal box and in a few days took charge. It was as if I had been 'on loan' to the Festiniog Railway.

The work was as busy as ever and the relief signalman who came to cover the other two shifts at the box felt that it ought to be up-graded. The 'marks' were duly taken and, mainly because of the shunting work we did, the box rose from a 'c' (the old 'Class 1') to a 'D', the highest grade box at Oxford and probably the highest grade mechanical box in the London Division. As I was sole, regular incumbent of the post this made me the top-class signalman at Oxford — manifestly untrue but technically a matter of fact. Accordingly, I would be certain of a place in the Panel signal box at Oxford when that installation was complete, late in 1973. The men who had wanted Hinksey North up-graded — this had never been my idea — were now upset that a sprig such as myself should be 'Number One for the Panel' before men with three or four times more service than I. These murmurings finally reached my ears and I was very happy to console the murmurers. Being particularly stupid where money and/or promotion is concerned, all these wranglings and calculations never occurred to me — I simply enjoyed being a hard-working, fairly expert, signalman in a very busy box. The realisation that I was first in line for a Panel job was alarming. I had visited Reading Panel on several occasions to see old friends incarcerated therein — several old friends had died from heart attacks after going to work in Reading and Swindon Panels — and everything I had learned about the Panel's workings from my time at Uffington and Kennington filled me with acute disdain for them. They went against everything that made being a signalman enjoyable; I would not be able to see the trains whilst I worked in a stressful, ugly, plastic environment. Panel boxes were definitely not for me and my occasionally absent-minded brain. Having broadcast this lengthy apologia over the 'bus-line' telephone the murmurings ceased, the seniorities of the men were again examined, my colleagues sorted themselves out into those who would go direct into the new Panel, those who would 'hang on until old so-and-so retires' and those who would take their redundancy pay and run. With the pecking order re-established I got broad-gauge smiles from my friends. They were welcome to their Panel.

Panel signal boxes are safe enough when everything is working normally. It seems to me that it is when the system is disrupted, either by accident or design, that matters are likely to go disastrously wrong. Matters often went dangerously wrong in semaphore signal boxes yet I always felt safer in one of these, in close, personal contact with the trains. It is when a Panel man mistakes an indication on his console or is forgetful and gives a driver incorrect or misunderstood instructions over the telephone that a train will go swanning off into the blue with no way of recalling it. There was insufficient communication between drivers and the Panel man and insufficient control over the trains.

During the night of 21/22 June 1970, for example, the down main line between Ashbury Crossing and Highworth Junction was blocked by engineering work and all trains between those places were running over the up main line. At about 6.15 a.m. on the 22nd, a down train passed through the cross-over points at Ashbury and travelled over the up main to Highworth Junction. Fred, in charge of the ground frame at Ashbury, took the 'G' clamp off the facing end of the cross-over and then walked to the telephone to ask Swindon Panel man what the next move would be. While Fred was talking on the telephone the down train was making swift progress over the 4½ miles to Highworth Junction. There it crossed back to the down main and dropped the Pilotman. That worthy walked across to the 2.10 a.m. Cardiff to Corby coal train and 'told the driver the tale': 'Single-line working between here and Ashbury over the up line. Obey all signals and look out for hand-signals from the men at the barriers and on the signal protecting the crossing at Ashbury. Right away.' The Cardiff set off at about 6.30 a.m. making a cracking pace with twenty-five tubs of coal and a guard's van behind diesel D1670.

By the time Fred had finished chatting on the phone to his mate in the Panel D1670 was in sight and the man protecting the road crossing was giving its driver a green flag to say that the public road was clear and safe for the train to cross. Fred had no time to get to the signal on the approach side of the crossing to give the driver a yellow signal — 'Caution' — which was the correct authorisation to the driver for him to pass at 'Danger' a three-aspect signal. Not that the yellow flag would have altered subsequent events. The driver took the green flag at the road crossing to mean that it was in order to pass the colour-light signal at 'Danger' — which was not the case — and the two men on the ground stood back as 600 tons of coal and steel thudded briskly past. Only one more train and they could both go home. Imagine, if you can, the feeling of 'bowels turning to water' felt by Fred when D1670 took a smart right and left through the cross-over and proceeded at increasing speed up the down main line. Fred had forgotten to put the cross-over back for straight running after the last down train.

The driver was by no means surprised at this sudden change of plan. He was used to and cynical of railway 'cock-ups' and decided that he had not been given proper instructions by the Pilotman. The thought that he was lustily compounding Fred's error never occurred to him and he drove happily onwards, up the down line. The two men on the ground bawled with all the power of their lungs at the guard as his van passed; he popped out of his caboose like a cork from a bottle, got the message and darted back inside to wind his hand-brake on and off as a means of attracting the driver's attention to the red flag he had placed over the side of the vehicle. In steam-hauled days this action with the brake would have had the effect of tugging the couplings back against the engine and the driver would undoubtedly have felt the 'bite' but the powerful diesel surged ahead quite impervious to the Victorian techniques of the guard in his equally Victorian, 20-ton brake-van. Anticipating that the train was not going to stop, Fred got into his car and drove through the lanes to Uffington, the site of the next set of cross-overs, in the hope that the train would stop there and he could then divert it back to the up main.

In Swindon Panel, the signalman and the District Inspector were watching the console. When the red, 'track-occupied' lights illuminated through the cross-over they thought they had a track-circuit failure but when the 'track failure' began to move eastwards they knew that they had a runaway on their hands. This caused them some concern because there was a 'light' engine running down the down main; it was then about six miles from the coal train and closing fast. The signalman decided that the engine would arrive at Uffington well before the coal train so he set the route for the engine to enter the down goods loop and thus clear the main line but the Inspector over-ruled him and told him to stop the engine at the first possible moment, at Baulking bridge, and, when the driver reported in on the signal post telephone, to ask him to go forward on foot to stop the driver of the coal train. The signalman therefore cancelled the route, the signal at Baulking bridge remained at 'Danger' but, as a consequence of the way the Panel system operates, the points remained set for the 'last called' position — into the loop.

While a certain tension developed in Swindon Panel, the District Inspector hurried to his car to follow Fred in the rush to Uffington, and the driver of the 2.10 a.m. Cardiff drove with perfect peace of mind over the road at Knighton crossing without benefit of protective barriers down against road traffic. In the Panel, the men gathered round the console to watch the progress of the red lights, towards each other, from west and east. As the lights continued to move they felt fairly sure that the coal train had not hit anything on the unguarded crossing. The next crisis was the spring-worked trailing point — now a facing point for a train running in the wrong direction — at the exit from Uffington goods loop. In normal single-line working conditions these would be clamped tightly in position with a 'G' clamp but, as matters stood on 22 June, they were entirely free and might well have been standing half open. There was a 20-ft drop off the embankment. The Panelmen stood helplessly and watched the red lights roll over the spring points and pass on. The driver — everyone concerned — had been very lucky, the whole train passed clear and came to a stand at the ground frame at Uffington facing the 'light' engine, 350 yards away at Baulking bridge. 'How long's this single-line working going on for?' the driver of the Cardiff asked Swindon Panelman on the phone as the second-man off the 'light' engine came running towards him holding a red flag.

Fred arrived shortly after, followed, fifteen minutes later, by the District Inspector. The coal train was standing on track circuits which prevented the Panelman giving the necessary electrical release to the ground frame key so the driver was told to reverse his train westwards 150 yards. No sooner had he started than there was a thudding and a jostling of wagons and four coal tubs were derailed. In the general confusion everyone had forgotten that the points were set to lead from down main to down loop and therefore the Cardiff had smashed them when it ran through them from the wrong direction.

That was the fault of the railwaymen aided by the inherent weakness of the system. The second Hungerford crash, like the first, was the fault of Management. It was only through sheer good fortune that there had not been more such incidents. The 12.45 a.m. Westbury to Theale on the night of 10 November 1971 consisted of forty-two 16-ton wagons loaded with stone and hauled by D1040 *Western Queen*. The train passed Woodborough box and gave the signalman there no cause for concern. Savernake and Bedwyn boxes were closed on night shift so the next box was Hungerford, over seventeen miles away and in this section the fourteenth wagon in the train

1 Reading (Southern) station, July 1931: a grimy 'K10' 4-4-0 heads a train of horse boxes and ancient carriages; the clock tower and platforms of the Great Western station appear in the background. This is how the author recalls the station in 1947

2 Woodley Bridge signal box in summer 1953 with a 'Castle' hurrying past with an up express from Bristol. Five years earlier the author had sat on the bridge in this very position and stared at the signalman until he had been invited into his box

3 Bill Kenning and his 1923 Riley at Challow after driving down from Sussex.
There is a can of Pratt's Motor Spirit on the running board and a bicycle
in case of serious breakdowns. His chimney-sweeping rods are partly covered
by a large collection of magpies' and crows' nests

4 A convivial evening with friends in Challow signal box, 1964: Bill Kenning
stands between Ron Price (r) and the author; Bill has the lever-pulling duster
over his shoulder

5 Uffington station, looking towards Challow, January 1962. The office block was built in 1863 in the post-Brunellian 'gloomy Gothic' style as the GWR's contribution to the Faringdon Railway. The signal box is late Victorian elegance. The Faringdon branch can be glimpsed behind the station nameboard

6 The sad scene from Uffington box, looking towards Challow, in 1966

7 The author's friends and colleagu[...]
Uffington from 1965 to 1968[...]
Spinage (*seated*) and Elwyn Rich[...]
Above Jim's head is the 1897 lig[...]
system which was still brought in[...]
in 1967 during power-cuts

8 Uffington's final layout from 14[...]
1966 until 3 March 1968 when [...]
don Panel signal box took [...]
(*above*) Ashbury siding (for P.[...]
Dept), automatic barriers and [...]
overs and Knighton barriers; (*b*[...]
Uffington loops and cross-over[...]
those at Challow. The villainous[...]
describer is on the right and [...]
of the hard-fought-for replac[...]
switches on the left

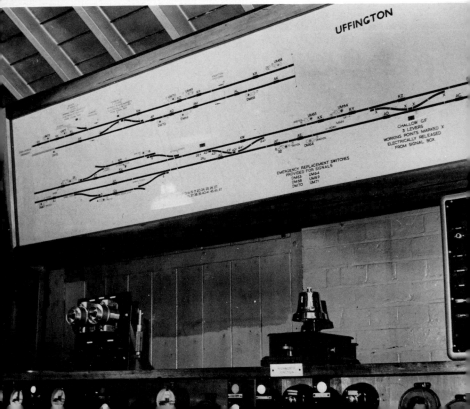

Conference at Uffington during single-line working, 1967: Inspector Charlie Sheppard (r) discusses the Pilotman's next move with Relief Signalman Cyril Thomas while Signalman Dennis Otterel looks at the camera and awaits instructions

The author at work in 1967: he acknowledges the train description code on the Highworth Junction bell—another up train has passed that place—while an up train is passing over the up loop facing points, an indication light being visible at that point on the diagram

11 The scene at Steventon, 22 September 1963, about 8 a.m. 6800 *Arlington Grange* is about to be re-railed after its driver drove it off the end of the down goods loop in the mistaken belief he was on the down main line. An express on the down main was stopped in the nick of time by Signalman Alec Abrahams

12 The scene one mile west of Uffington signal box, 7 January 1966, about 8 a.m. The aftermath of the crash when the two wagons pictured, loaded with pig-iron, broke axles and crashed onto the track

...nnington Junction signal box in ...68: 1901-pattern lever frame and ...1961 train describer; next to this ...the traditional bell on which emer-...ncy codes were exchanged with ...ading Panel—the bell was also ...ed to send/receive train description ...des when the describer failed

...nnington Junction signal box from ...e branch line in 1968: the top arm ...the down branch home signal with ...nksey South's distant signal below. ...e short arm routes trains to the ...wn goods loop. The figure '20' ...ninds drivers of the permitted ...eed across the junction. The near-...points are set for the up loop to ...otect the main line against the ...nger of a runaway off the branch

15 A peaceful Sunday morni[ng at]
Kennington, 1969. The c[ ]
of a 'D63' class diesel m[ ]
out his time-sheet. The M[ ]
Cowley branch electric t[ ]
instrument is in the [ ]
ground, with the wil[ ]
swamp in the distance

16 Looking south at Kennin[g]
towards Didcot, 1969: a '[ ]
stands quietly on the br[ ]
line while Traffic and [Per-]
manent-Way Dept staff s[ ]
absorbed, watching other[ ]
prepare to weld a join[t be-]
tween two rails

17 The view north from Hinksey North signal box in 1970: the rear of the 9.15 a.m. Paddington is passing over the points from down loop to down main while a 'Hymek' hauls the Littlemore oil train out of South End Yard and over the Thames Bridge on the up goods loop

18 Hinksey North box interior looking north, 1970: levers 60 to 1 can be seen. The road is set 'field-side up' at the far end; the two nearer levers work the bolts in facing points from up main to down reception and up loop No 2

19 The view south from Hinksey North, in 1970, with the No 1 up loop starting signal lowered on the gantry and a 'unique' train on the down loop: nearest the camera, 30777 *Sir Lamiel*, next 30925 *Cheltenham*, 30120 and 50621. They were being hauled to the National Railway Museum at York but 30777 'escaped' and, as No 777, is once again earning hard cash for British Rail

20 Looking north from Hinksey South box in 1972 as a pair of Class 20 diesels free-wheel a 'Merry-go-Round' coal train for Didcot power station into the up goods loop to clear the up main for a following express

21 Hinksey South box, looking south from the yard, 1973: the South and North boxes were identical in appearance. The rail-car is coasting on the up main line, passing Kennington Junction's distant signal at 'Caution'

22 The Clink road passed over a broad-gauge railway arch at Clink Road Junction. The signals are lowered for a train to go into Frome—Clink Road Junction's starting signal and Frome North's distant signal. Taken at 6.15 a.m. on 21 June 1974, one of the rare occasions when the sun shone on the face of the signals and cast shadows on the bridge

23 Posed for effect, a movement that would never, normally, arise. These two trains approached the junction simultaneously. The author stopped them both and then crossed the Class 33 into Frome *en route* for Whatley quarry. The other is a loaded stone train from Merehead quarry

24 31296 hauls the 10.5 a.m. Weymouth to Bristol past Frome North box (built *c.* 1875) on 14 June 1975. The train is running on the Blatchbridge–Frome single track; double track starts a few yards further on

25 Tom Baber at ease in Frome North signal box, 1975. The traditional signal box tasting fork, a fine example, hand-made by some long-dead signalman, is conveniently placed, ready for instant use

26 'Tiny' Fred Wilkins does not have to stretch to hand the Merehead branch token to the driver of 1068 *Western Reliance* as it goes down to the quarry with empty trucks on 5 June 1975

27 Low summer sunlight casts
dows and catches the brass
on the Merehead quarry b
token instrument in Witham
The telephone to the Quarry
tion ground frame is on th
and the hooped token carrie
hanging by the GWR clock.
are several tokens in the in
ment, one is raised on edge

28 The 3.30 p.m. Paddington h
past Witham box, 'in the c
trailing a plume of black s
In the foreground the up b
home signal has two arm
right hand directing trains
up main, the other along a b
loop

29 The weather was not always sunny. On 14 July 1975 a sudden thunderstorm brought torrential rain. Looking out through the rain-blurred windows of Witham box the author saw 1012 *Western Firebrand* on the 8.45 a.m. Penzance which had gained one minute on a tight schedule climbing Brewham bank in the downpour

30 Signalman Vaughan entertains a trespasser in Witham box—his mother, a dyed-in-the-wool GWR enthusiast. His father took the photograph so that made two trespassers one afternoon in February 1975

31 A typically busy morning at Witham—although the author managed to spare a few minutes to record the scene. On the left, on the branch loop, 33003 waits for the single line to clear so that it can go down to Cranmore with those tanks. 1040 *Western Queen* on a Westbury to Yeovil special goods has been shunted to the up main rather than the down siding to clear the line for the 9.30 a.m. Paddington, hurrying through on 8 August 1975

developed a hot-axle bearing. Half a mile before it reached Hungerford the trailing right-hand axle bearing broke and the wagon rolled on at around 40 mph, rocking about a diagonal axis as the load was carried on the leading right-hand and trailing left-hand wheels. A few seconds later the 12.35 a.m. Paddington to Plymouth express passed and its driver, seeing the flames and sparks, blew a warning on his horn to the guard of the train. Guard Harvey put his head over the side, saw the trouble and was going back to get a red light when the engine braked suddenly, causing him to be knocked off balance and rendered unconscious.

Up in Hungerford box, the signalman, Robbie Bowden, had seen the flames and sparks and had thrown his signals to 'Danger'. He was just about to send 'Obstruction Danger' to Kintbury when the derailed fourteenth wagon crashed through the signal box and Robbie, too, lost consciousness. The expertise of the local Fire Brigade was required to extricate him from the total wreck of his box. The remarkable thing was that he was still alive. He was away from work for nineteen days and told me later that the whole episode had been a waking nightmare. Twenty-six wagons were overturned, blocking up and down main lines but the fourteen leading wagons with the engine broke away and remained on the rails as did the last three, including the brake van. Of the fourteen all were found to be overloaded — on average by $3\frac{3}{4}$ tons, the worst case was wagon 555592, 7 tons 1 cwt over the limit. It is reasonable to assume that the others were also overloaded but whether the crash was caused primarily by this or by a primary lack of oil in the bearing will remain a mystery. Western Region had to replace half a mile of track, build a new signal box and clear up the mess. All this was an unavoidable expense but the need for a weighbridge could not be proved conclusively so, six years after the first crash and six months after the 'second, Western Region was still agonising over whether or not to incur the expense of moving a redundant weighbridge from Wednesbury to a suitable site in the Westbury area.

Reducing the expensive infrastructure was the order of the day. One Saturday night in the autumn of 1971 I was booked for a ten-hour shift till 8 a.m. on Sunday, 'on the ground', at Didcot North Junction. There was no shelter on the embankment so it was usual to get a car on to the track bed of the old up goods loop at Appleford and drive to the signal at the junction. The Inspector in charge had come to the site with his car which, being generally more luxurious than mine, he kindly invited me to share. The engineers were going to re-lay some track and had to lift the old, timber-sleepered sections out before putting down the concrete-sleepered sections. Normally a powerful steam or diesel crane would have been used for this work but as a result of the policy of reducing the expensive infrastructure — in this case scrapping cranes — the work was to proceed using a hired crane, mounted on a road-lorry. As an old-hand once said, 'The blessed road gets in everywhere.'

My job was to see that the crane was not swinging lengths of track through the air when a train was approaching. This involved liaising with the Panel, trudging about on the ballast, giving instructions to the workmen and trying to stay awake by drinking a lot of horrible, thermos-flask tea. After about five hours out in the dark and the cold, with my stomach audibly awash with tea, the train service slackened to the usual 'small hours' emptiness so the Inspector and I sought relaxation and warmth in the plush confines of his car.

With the interior light on, the windows were just black, mirroring our tired faces. We shared sandwiches as the wind moaned and buffeted the car, rocking it slightly in the gusts. As we ate we talked about steam days and retirement days. For him the latter were close at hand and he told me how he was looking forward to living in Bournemouth and playing his trombone in a dance band. We grew wearier and his hopes and the anecdotes about the old days faded into a grumble about the present woes of Western Region. It had, according to my Inspector, a lot to do with the 'foreigners' who were — and had been for some time — in charge at Paddington.

'All these blokes off the LNER, they come, stir it all up and clear off, leaving someone else to sort out the mess. They've no manners. A couple or three years ago Gerry Fiennes wanted the Reading–London suburban service improved. Poor old Bill Noke was put in charge of it, him and some others. They sorted out new workings for men, rail cars, engines — it took a long time and before they had the job properly thought through Fiennes comes roaring along demanding that they have the scheme in place for May. Bill said it would be ready for September but Fiennes said "May" so on it went, a right-old mess and Bill Noke got the blame for it. All cuts and cock-ups on this railway.' We were interrupted in our pleasantly gloomy task of tearing 'foreigners' to shreds by a knock on the window. The Inspector wound down the glass, let in the gale and the face of the Permanent-Way Inspector. 'We'll be finished soon.'

'How's that then? The occupation was till eight o'clock. You haven't got it all relaid already, have you?'

'You must be joking. The road-lorry crane couldn't lift the concrete sections. It nearly folded in two when it took the strain. I phoned the Divisional Engineer, got him out of bed at about three o'clock — it's his clever idea to have a road crane. He told me to cut the concrete sections in half so the crane can lift them.'

'Eh!?' said my Inspector. 'You can't do that, we'll be here for days, cutting and drilling.'

'Well, that's what I told him. So he said to put all the old stuff back in until we can get hold of a proper crane — so that's what we've been doing and now we're back where we started and you can go home.'

I once worked three twelve-hour night shifts at Old Oak Common as a hand-signalman while a large-scale rearrangement of the layout took place. I went up to Paddington by passenger train and rode down to Old Oak on the first available empty coaching stock train so that, with travelling time in each direction, the shifts were more like sixteen hours each. Men from all over the London Division were drafted in. It was good to be in a 'gang' and to hear the news from High

Wycombe and Newbury before we split up to go to our respective signal posts. In the darkness the world was one of disembodied lights. The rails gleamed red from signal lamps or white from arc lights at the site of work. Invisible streets were traced by lines or orange sodium lamps; the lattice-work of the great bridge carrying the West London line over the main line was silhouetted against the starry sky and looked like the work of Titans. I stood at a signal post between the main and relief lines, ear clamped to the telephone when the huge diesels came grumbling, rumbling, lumbering along, grinding to a stand, towering overhead as I stood in the 'valley' between the heaped ballast of each track. I asked 'Is Line Clear?' of the Panelman and, stretching up as high as I could to reach the hand-rails, climbed the cab steps to shout instructions in the driver's ear above the steady, throbbing hammer of his engine. I clambered down and stood, collar turned up against a nasty, cutting breeze as the dark shapes that made up the train drummed past, the diesel's exhaust a howling, black plume against the deepest, navy-blue sky.

By midnight on the third night of what were virtually sixteen-hour shifts I was very tired. Around two o'clock that morning the chill wind carried the cries of a prisoner in Wormwood Scrubs, 600 yards away across a playing field, distant but clearly audible — 'Help me, help me' — over and over again until the voice ceased. I have never forgotten that desolate sound heard on the buffeting wind as the pain in my guts caused by tiredness grew, unassuaged by coffee or sandwiches. By 3 a.m. I was ready to drop. Quite when I did drop I cannot recall but it had no effect on the trains. I woke, shivering, chilled to the bone, lying full length on the ballast, a grey dawn breaking and the trains roaring past, a couple of feet away from my head.

After a long weekend experiencing the virtues of a mid-Victorian regime as a lineside policeman without the latter's physical fitness, it was sheer luxury to return to Hinksey North, the fire, the armchair and sixty-nine highly polished levers. The box was off the beaten track and I had only one railway enthusiast visitor all the time I worked there. At least, he said he was a railway enthusiast. He was a pleasant lad of about thirteen in the uniform of a well-known Oxford college school. He called up from the path, asking if he could come in and, of course, I let him. He asked sensible questions and I was quite pleased with him. The following week he came again and asked questions about the opening and closing times of signal boxes on the Worcester line. Well, I thought he wanted to visit them when they were open so I gave him the working timetable and he made a copy of their times and went away. I never saw him again.

The weekend passed and the following Monday night I was watching television, waiting to go on night shift when there was a loud knock on the front door. I opened it and found two large men in civilian clothes, one of whom was holding out a piece of paper. 'This is a search warrant,' he intoned. 'We have reason to believe there is stolen property in this house.' Stunned, I stood aside and let them in. The man with the search warrant then said he wanted to meet one Adrian Vaughan and, alarmed and totally mystified, I identified myself. 'We believe you have a quantity of railway signalling equipment stolen from signal boxes on the Worcester line during the weekend,' the voluble one said. The other fixed me with a professional, fishy stare. I had not been to work since Saturday noon and so I knew nothing at all about this burglary. Up in my room I did have a quantity of signalling equipment which I had taken into protective custody when the box concerned was being closed, much of the stuff I had actually used when it was in situ.

'What exactly are you looking for?' I asked, my voice trembling enough for it to show. The one with the stare silently produced a list. They were doing their best to be intimidating — and they were succeeding. I looked at it in growing amazement, someone had stripped out instruments and clocks from working signal boxes.

'But I haven't got any of this stuff — there's enough here to open a railway — I've nowhere to put it all — I'm a signalman,

I'd never do such a thing,' my protests came tumbling out, urged on by anxiety.

'You were seen,' said the voluble policeman, scenting an arrest from my nervousness. 'Your car was seen at all these places on Sunday morning.'

'And you'd know when these boxes were closed, wouldn't you?' said the hitherto silent one. But I knew they were lying. Someone had suggested they try me, a shot in the dark because I was an enthusiastic railwayman, they were just trying it on.

I became confident, even angry. 'Any railwayman would know when those boxes were shut and it wasn't me that broke into them. Look, I've got some stuff upstairs, you'd better come and see but there's nothing on your list.'

As we went up the dark, narrow stairs I suddenly remembered the well-mannered little boy with the angelic face, short trousers and a desire to know about the closing times of the Worcester line boxes. Could he be behind this, the cause of my present predicament and maybe the cause of my losing my treasured relics? I opened the door of my room and the two officers plunged in like labradors diving into a pond to retrieve a shot duck. There was nothing in my possession that was on the list — my stuff was much better quality — and after I explained to them that I held my souvenirs from boxes I had worked or known well, out of a love of the job, they very decently let the matter drop.

In September 1970 I was driving a Wolsley 1500. I had a GWR locomotive vacuum gauge fixed to the dashboard and a length of plastic tube from it to the carburettor. The 8-in. diameter gauge came to life and registered a vacuum when the engine was running so I could adjust the throttle to get the greatest economy from the engine whilst running — about 45 mpg. I filled the tank with a measured gallon and drove till the fuel ran out to ensure correct consumption figures. Driving out of Oxford one evening, west along Botley Road, I saw on the pavement ahead a pair of very trim ankles and legs stepping briskly along. There was a brown coat down which tumbled a lot of curly, auburn hair and, sticking out at right-angles, was the right arm, dainty thumb raised. I stopped. She was going to Wantage. So was I. She got in. By the top of Cumnor Hill I knew her name was Susan. I also knew I ought to ask her for a date. By the Greyhound at Besselsleigh I knew I dared not ask, she was about seventeen to my twenty-nine. At Frilford golf course my measured gallon ran out. 'I'm afraid we've run out of petrol,' I said apologetically. She looked out at the wide open spaces in the evening sun and turned to look daggers at me down her rather haughty nose. I saw how very green were her eyes. She was reaching for the door handle.

'Don't worry,' I reassured her hastily, 'I've a gallon in the back — look.' I showed her my big, brass, GWR vacuum gauge, explained what I was trying to do and she relaxed knowing that I was merely a harmless conserver of energy and not the local nutcase. Half a dozen times during that journey I nearly asked her to come out for the evening and to prolong our journey together I drove her to her front door. Just as she was getting out of the car I blurted out the question. 'Yes, all right,' she answered, quite simply and easily. I was so sure that this was an event of the greatest importance that I made a note of the meeting on the fly-leaf of Volume 1 of McDermott's *History of the Great Western Railway*.

Very shortly after this my digs in Abbey Road came under new management when the man of the house and his mate a few doors down the street amicably swapped wives whilst the children of each family stayed in their original homes but visited their mothers, a matter of some confusion to the children. The new wife was bulkily pregnant and after a gallant struggle she found she could not cope and asked if I would mind leaving. I left at once. She was a very nice girl but a shocking cook, not to be compared with her predecessor. The weather was gloriously autumnal. I had a fine, ex-RAF sleeping bag so I rearranged the interior of the Wolsley and took to sleeping in the car, parked up a pleasant lane, and to cooking by the roadside. After a couple of weeks I found lodgings in north Oxford, in a garret — literally — at the top of a Victorian house owned by a tea-cosy-shaped Jewish refugee from Austria, Mrs Morgenstern. She had three other tenants: a German of extreme timidity who worked in the darkest, most esoteric bookshop in a city full of such things; a Bristolian called 'Cissul' (in the 'Bristle' vernacular); and a shy Irishman. So now I was 'doing' for myself again, cycling along Walton Street to work and cutting my own sandwiches. Susan came straight from school to visit me in the box when I was on late turn but I could never persuade her to so much as tap out a code on the block bell; she was happy to sit and do her homework or read until it was time to leave. If I finished at ten o'clock I took her home but if I finished at six o'clock we would go out into the town to see a film or go to the Playhouse and then back to my garret with a take-away. No matter how stealthily we crept into the house these visits were always known to Mrs Morgenstern and she always rang down the curtain in the same way and at the same time. I can hear her now, her discreet, Viennese accent floating softly up the long flights of stairs: 'Yoo-hoo . . . it's ten-thirty!'

CHAPTER EIGHT

ACCIDENTS AVERTED

Every signalman should shudder at the name of Quintinshill. This was the site of the worst accident in the long history of accidents on Britain's railways. It took place on 22 May 1915, and was the result of a signalman's forgetfulness. He had shunted a down troop train to the up line to allow a faster, following, train to pass. While he was waiting for this to take place he was talking to various railwaymen who had accumulated in his box, including the fireman of the troop train. In spite of the presence of the latter and the fact of the troop train standing right outside the window on the up line, the signalman lowered his signal for an up express and in the subsequent, head-on, collision 216 people were killed. Chatter between railwaymen in a signal box was commonplace; accidents as a result of it were rare, yet friendly conversation provided a potential distraction and to that extent it was dangerous. When the distraction coincided with some other factor there was a disaster. Oh, the convoluted interactions of fate which must combine to cause a crash! When they do, the signalman's feelings are extremely unpleasant. I confess I know them well.

I was enjoying the usual, busy, morning at Hinksey North. The day was fine and summery in 1970 and I was happy on the bells, levers, instruments and telephones. The Pilot was shunting to and fro over the river bridge, the signals were 'off' for the 9.15 a.m. Paddington to Oxford express and a 'light' diesel was on its way to me from Hinksey South via the down goods loop. It arrived outside the box with Didcot men on board.

' "Light" back to Didcot, Bobby,' said the driver cheerfully.

'You can go out behind the down London,' I replied. 'Out onto the bridge and cross over behind the 10.30 Oxford up.'

'There's time to make some tea, then,' said the driver and, turning to his secondman, added, 'Go up and sign the book, make some tea and I'll pick you up after he's crossed us over.'

I knew the secondman, Ron, very well from steam days. He signed on the train register and remained in the box as a reminder to me that his engine was standing (or would shortly be standing) on the down main line. Soon we were reminding each other about our 'steam days' exploits. The 9.15 Paddington passed down the main, I gave 'Train out of Section' — 2–1 on the bell — to Johnny Blanchard at Hinksey South who promptly 'asked the road' — 3–2–5 on the bell — for a 'Freightliner'. I gave the road. A minute later the 9.15 Paddington cleared Oxford Station South box so I 'asked on' for the 'Freightliner'. Arthur Lane gave me 'Line Clear' and 'asked the road', 3-1 on the bell, for the 10.30 a.m. Oxford on the up main. I pulled off for this train but did not pull off for the 'Freightliner'. Instead I reversed the points from down loop to down main and told the driver to go ahead, stop on the bridge and wait there to cross over.* This movement did not foul the 'clearing point' of my down home signal so it was correct.

The 10.30 Oxford did not leave the station on time; Ron and I carried on our conversation and in those two minutes or so the element of forgetfulness crept in. Suddenly the down-line instruments caught my eye, showing 'Line Clear'. I remembered the 'Freightliner', said, 'Damn, I've forgotten to pull off for the Lawley Street,' and promptly did so. I turned from the levers to walk back to my desk — and saw the engine standing peacefully on the bridge, the driver reading his newspaper and, dangling like a Sword of Damocles above his head, my down-main starting signal at 'All Right'. Yelling something utterly unprintable to relieve the surge of panic I felt, I slammed the three levers back into the frame. The down line signals had been lowered for about five seconds.

Ron's tea mug stopped half-way to his mouth as he watched the frantic flurry of pulling-off and throwing-back accompa-

---

* See D on diagram on p. 88.

nied with much bad language. 'What's up?' he asked mildly.

I had given myself a bad scare and I vented my feelings on him. 'What are you supposed to be here for?' I snapped in a very bad temper.

'Well, I dunno, mate, Rule 55 I suppose,' he stammered, embarrassed.

'And what have I just done?'

'Well, I dunno, mate — I'm not a signalman, am I?'

'I'm not too certain if I am either,' I said ruefully. 'I've just pulled off for the "Freightliner" with your mate sitting out there reading the sports pages.'

'Oo, I'm sugared,' said Ron nervously, 'you'd better put 'em back then, hadn't you?'

'I already have,' I replied, feeling very weary, 'but that just goes to show what talking can do.'

The 10.30 Oxford went by four minutes later; I crossed the engine to the up main and lowered the signals for the Lawley Street. When the driver stopped opposite the box to pick up Ron I asked him if he had seen anything odd about the signals. 'Well, funny thing — I glanced up to see if you'd pulled the dummy* and I thought I saw the main-line boards off. I did a double-take but they were "on". Queer though.'

The Southampton–Lawley Street 'Freightliner' went by at that moment, belching black smoke, as the 'Brush' diesel worked back into speed from a signal check and, when the long line of containers had drummed past, my mates were up at the starting signal, 'waiting the road home'.

Hinksey North, being close to the Thames, was very susceptible to fogs. One October morning the mist rose till it was 'thick as a bag' and visibility was down to 25 yards. At 10.15 the place was full of trains. The shunters were trying to marshal one for Morris Cowley, the engine for which was waiting on the up goods loop. The return trip from Abingdon was waiting at the signal on the down reception line, where it had been for half an hour, awaiting the shunters' pleasure —

---

* Ground signal.

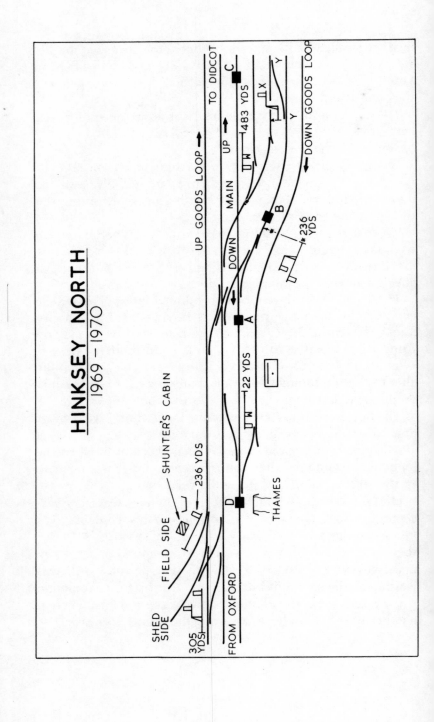

HINKSEY NORTH
1969 – 1970

SHED SIDE

FIELD SIDE

SHUNTER'S CABIN

305 YDS

236 YDS

FROM OXFORD

THAMES

D

A

B

C

22 YDS

236 YDS

483 YDS

UP GOODS LOOP

DOWN

MAIN

UP

DOWN GOODS LOOP

TO DIDCOT

W

W

W

X

Y

Y

out of sight and out of mind. A 'light' engine was groping its way around the edge of Hinksey yard on the down goods loop with the intention of hooking on to a train of coal for Bletchley. To reach the train the engine would have to go out onto the down main line at the bridge and reverse up the down line, on to the down reception and thence to the yard. (See opp.) The next train on the down main would be the 9.15 a.m. Paddington but the fog had made it late and it was not signalled.

The engine on the down loop, a 'Brush' diesel, emerged from the fog and stopped under the box window. I slid the window back to give the driver his instructions. Beyond in the murk I could hear the savage snatch of couplings and the grinding, howling sound peculiar to a diesel shunter's gears and engine. To the driver of the 'light' diesel I said, 'Your train's on Number One in the down yard. I've set the road onto the down main, go by the loop starter at "Danger" and stop on the bridge. When you see the dummy there come off, you'll know you have the road all the way to the yard. But listen — be sure you blow three honks each time you clear points so I'll know when to move them. I can't see a thing from here.'

Apart from the dense fog all this was routine at Hinksey North; the driver nodded and set off. Three honks came, muffled, through the fog so I set the road for the down yard and, as I did so, Johnny Blanchard 'asked the road' for the 9.15 Paddington. I 'refused' the train because the movement I was about to make would reverse within the clearing point of the down home signal. The 'Brush' diesel slid very slowly past the box, looking almost black in the fog. There was a definite tension involved in the operation; the driver and I exchanged stiff little nods and waves as I stood anxiously at the window and he inched his engine cautiously along the track. The dense fog was a kind of daylight nightmare. I remained at the window and tried to visualise the engine's progress along the rails, attempting to keep some idea of what was happening so as to work the box as effectively as possible.

After a full two minutes I heard three long blasts on a diesel's horn. This was about the right time-interval to allow the engine to clear off the main line so I threw the dummy and points back to normal, gave 'Line Clear' for the 9.15 Paddington and pulled off. As I pulled my distant signal a ghastly thought went through my head like an electric shock: Which engine had blown? Was it the engine I was shunting or the one waiting on the up goods loop, impatient to be let into the yard? Then I remembered the Abingdon standing at the down reception line signal. There was no track-circuit reminder nor even a signalling instrument, the line was signalled over the telephone and an entry made in the train register. It must have been the driver of the Abingdon blowing a warning to the driver of the approaching 'Brush'. All this realisation went through my head, literally, at the speed of light. I flung the signals back to 'Danger', rushed to the bell and sent 'Obstruction Danger' to Johnny Blanchard. There was silence and I knew, from the time since he first 'asked the road' for the express, that it must be close to him and therefore the silence meant that he was busy, throwing his signals back to 'Danger' to stop the train. I waited on tenterhooks for several — long — seconds. If he replied to my 6 bells with 6 bells it meant he had succeeded in stopping it but if he had been unable to stop it I would receive 4–5–5 'Train running away on the right line'. I got 4–5–5 and felt sick.

I stood rooted to the floor, weighing the chances of a crash, the site of which was too far away for me to be able to intervene in the time available. The driver of the 9.15 would have seen my outer distant, just south of Hinksey South, at 'All Right' but he would certainly have had my inner, north of Hinksey South, at 'Caution' — but was this sufficient braking distance for him to be able to stop at my home signal? About 150 yards ahead of my home signal was a stationary engine, maybe a derailed engine, because I must have moved those points when it was very close to them. These thoughts went through my head as I stood at the open window.

I stared into the fog, my face as cold and as pale as the mist. I could hear the steady knocking of a diesel engine but otherwise nothing. Then there were footsteps and the driver of the 'light' engine came running out of the fog and up the box stairs, two at a time. He was angry. 'Hey! What's going on? You all but had us off the road — and there's a train on the down reception. Didn't you know that? It blew-up at me, otherwise I wouldn't have been able to stop in time.' In the fog his nerves had been stretched, this had set them vibrating like the E string of a violin.

I sat down on the edge of the table, feeling like a deflated balloon; he must have seen this or read it in my face because his attitude softened. 'Are you all right? Did you know about that one on the down reception?'

'I ought to have known about it,' I replied miserably. 'I booked it into the register but it's been there for so long that I forgot about it. I heard it blowing at you and took that as your "inside clear" signal.'

'Well, at least you're honest about it, but what now?'

Through the fog came the prolonged braying of a diesel's horn.

'That's what,' I said. 'That's the 9.15 Padd — when I thought you were clear of the down main I gave the road for it. I hope they can stop.'

'You'll bloody soon know,' said the driver with some feeling. There was another long bray and then silence. 'They've stopped,' said the driver, his voice rising on each word.

Once the tension was broken I found I was shaking and not much use for anything. The driver, less shocked, took charge. 'Right', he said crisply, 'here's what we do.' He leant forwards towards me and gripped my arm as he spoke. 'This fog's so thick that the men on the fast don't know what's happened. I'll bring my engine back onto the down loop before they get off their engine and come up here. When I'm on the loop you can pull off and we'll be squared-up.'

He hurried away leaving me feeling utterly disappointed with myself and sad at the thought that this was probably the end of my signalling career. But when the engine was safely back on my down loop my spirits rose. I pulled off for the 9.15 Paddington and three minutes later a big 'Western' class diesel was grinding to a halt outside, its driver sliding back his cab window. I walked to the window knowing that my future depended on how I handled the driver, on his mood.

'What's on today then, officer?' was his grim opening. 'I got your outer "off" and your inner went back in my face with Hinksey South's starter. One second of delay and I'd have passed it at "All Right".' He had had a very nasty shock in virtually zero visibility at 75 mph and he looked accusingly at me, awaiting my answer.

'Well, it's a bit of a long story, driver. I really am very sorry you were given such a bad fright in this filthy fog but everything is fine, nothing to worry about.' My heart was pounding, I was dying for him to go away and I pointed diplomatically at my lowered starting signal. 'You've got the road, everything's fine.' We looked directly into each other's eyes at a range of forty feet. I met and held his gaze for a long moment, then, very deliberately, he said, 'We depend on you buggers.' I spread my hands out: 'I'm sorry.' He slid his window shut, revved the huge engine and drew the train away.

I felt fairly sure he would not report the incident, there was nothing really for him to report, looking at it from his point of view — a signalman's job is to stop trains — but he still had an inkling that something had gone wrong. My spirits rose again and I got on with the job but after a while I felt depressed once more and telephoned the District Inspector to ask him to come to the box.

'I'm rather busy,' he said, 'can't you come to see me when you finish?'

'No, I think I'd like you here now.'

'Oh dear,' he said, 'I don't think I like the sound of that. I'll be along to you in a few minutes.' Ten minutes later he came hurrying up the track and into the signal box. I told him what had happened, showed him all my entries in the register and waited to hear my sentence. 'Well, all right, you made a genuine mistake. I think you were pretty good to get out of it so quickly. You took the right action as soon as you realised what you'd done.' I could have wrung his hand from his wrist at that moment but he was already leaving. 'Must press on — got a lot to do,' he said, and clattered down the stairs.

In mid-1970 work began on the rebuilding of Oxford station. The platforms were dismantled — half their length at any one time — and the fine old wooden office buildings, dating back to Brunel and 1852, were pulled down. Naturally I felt that restoration, not vandalism, was needed. While the platforms were reduced in length, posters displayed at Paddington, Reading and Didcot warned passengers to get out of a train from the front or rear five coaches depending on which bit of platform was missing. Loudspeaker announcements were made, guards and ticket collectors also spread the warning. Thousands were saved from hurling themselves to perdition — all but one. At 7 p.m. one dark night, a down express arrived from London and the driver skilfully brought his train to a stand with the rear coaches alongside the northern half of the down platform. This placed the leading coach on the canal bridge. In the leading compartment of this coach were some Oxford locomotivemen going home and a Canadian on business. When the train stopped the locomotivemen trooped out into the corridor, the first man opened the door, stepped out onto the flat-topped girder of the bridge and, turning sharp right, walked along it to the footpath at the far end. The other railwaymen followed, all knowing exactly what they were doing in the deep darkness, all with equally steely nerves above the black water. Bringing up the rear came the Canadian. He went through the door, stepped onto the bridge — and into space.

He did not have a terribly long way to fall, 15 ft or so, but he probably thought he was falling forever and went down yelling. The departing locomotivemen heard his cries and the enormous splash, realised what had happened and rushed to his aid. I believe one man went so far as actually to get into the water. The innocent Canadian was not in the least bit impressed by such a sacrifice and once on dry land was soon glowing in the heat of his own indignation. The story went through the signal boxes almost as fast as he had fallen into the water. If he had heard the gales of laughter it provoked I think he would have died of apoplexy.

When the station was complete, early in 1972, it consisted of what looked to me like a collection of upmarket porta-cabins inadequately sheltered by a steel and aluminium awning filched from a petrol filling station. The impression I received was that my employers were neither looking for nor hoping for an increase in traffic; on the contrary, they were saying 'We surrender' in brick and plywood whilst cowering under a petrol filling station canopy. Together with this blow, the new Panel signal box at Oxford was due to come into service in October 1973 — the shape of things to come was before me and March 1972 seemed like a good time for making far-reaching decisions.

Susan and I decided to get married in June and I decided to leave the railway as soon as possible. Susan was a cog in Robert Maxwell's Pergamon Press, working as a sub-editor on four scientific journals one of which was in Russian Cyrillic script so she never knew if she had 'subbed' it correctly. I had had two small picture books published by the fledgling Oxford Publishing Company so printing/publishing seemed to be the way forward. In June I put my signalman's duster down on the levers and took a job with the aptly named family printing firm of Parchment. Shortly after this Susan and I were married. I have bitterly regretted that my occupation is given on the marriage certificate as 'storeman' rather than 'signalman'.

We went to live in my bachelor garret. The roof sloped so steeply down on one side that we had to stand, back against the other wall in order to be able to stand up right to pull on our clothes. All our worldly goods — old signalling instruments for the most part — were shoved under the bed. Marriage was a great success, and, indeed, continues to be so fifteen years later but the decision taken during the Ides of March regarding another job was an unmitigated disaster. By 10.30 each morning I was yawning enough to dislocate my jaw and by eleven o'clock I was hard pressed to stay awake. It was only embarrassment that prevented me from going at once to lurk nonchalantly outside the District Inspector's door. Don Parchment, ex-Paratroop Sergeant-Major, ex-Chindit, was remarkably patient and never failed to pay me my wages though I never earned a penny for him and sometimes caused him great loss. A touch of the button on the hydraulic guillotine and 500 sheets of glossy art paper, 2 ft by 3 ft, were cut the wrong way round. Even after such waste as this he never became angry, well, not for an ex-Sergeant-Major but after eight weeks the weight on my conscience and the sheer, pressing need to get back into a signal box overcame my embarrassment at returning to the fold so quickly. The District Inspector was very kind and sent me to Hinksey South immediately. I had hoped for Hinksey North but had forgotten that the box was at the top of the wages scale and was therefore not available to a recruit 'straight off the street'.

My goodness, I was glad to be back among signal bells and signal levers! Hinksey South was built at the same time as the North box and was identical to look at. It stood on the up side of the line about 100 yards north of the old Abingdon Road bridge. It had a frame of fifty-eight levers numbered 1 to 72, to work goods loops, main lines and Hinksey Up Yard. The latter had been shut in 1970, although some small amount of work was still done on its sidings, and a month after I arrived the points from up loop to up main were damaged and not repaired. Luckily for the look of the thing, the signal on the gantry applying to that route was not removed. The train service was busy; any morning between 7 and 8.30 a train would pass the box every 4½ minutes and there would be ninety-three trains in the course of a 6 a.m. to 2 p.m. shift. Although this was as many trains as had run thirty years before the work was less exacting because the yard was shut; all I had to do was to pass the trains along the track from Kennington to Hinksey North with some small amount of goods train regulating.

Of especial importance were up goods trains which were

booked relief on the up avoiding line at Didcot: was the fresh set of men available; could the train stop to change crews without delaying a following passenger train? The difficulty was created by the skeletal nature of the layout at Didcot since automation. Sometimes Reading Panel, sometimes 'Control', let the Hinksey man know what was required; if not I would make my own inquiries and, if necessary, divert the goods to the loop as the last 'lay-by' on the up main before Didcot East Junction's up relief line.

On 15 August 1973 the 4069 'Freightliner' went up a few minutes early. I therefore had made no inquiries about its relief at Didcot. It came to a stand at a green signal at the south end of the avoiding line and the driver went to the signal post telephone. 'Five-thirty Lawley Street here. Got our relief about?'

The Reading Panelman had thought that 4069 on his describer was a mistake. 'You don't run today,' he told the driver. 'My notice here has you down, "Will not run" today but "Will run" tomorrow, so there's no relief for you.'

'Well,' said the driver, 'my notice has us down as "Will run" today and "Will not run" tomorrow and I want my relief today.'

The train was inter-Regional, LMR to SR via WR, and a confusion had arisen in spite of all the 'high-tech' communications. This blocked the up avoiding line for an hour or so while a spare set of men were found and sent to Didcot. Next day the booked Southern men turned up at Didcot but of course the LMR did not run the train.

On 5 September 1973 a colour-light signal was erected outside the signal box, a few feet from the window. Several weeks previously the engineers had drilled a hole in the ground with an auger and dropped into it a 40-gallon, empty oil drum which they then filled with cement from a rail-borne mixer. Four long bolts, from the bottom of the drum to about 9 in. above it, were held in a square formation by a timber framing which also acted as a 'former' for the above-ground portion of the cement. On the 5th five men arrived in a three-ton lorry. They had with them various fittings to make a signal, a hired ladder and a length of rope. They broke the timber away from the concrete and bolt threads and laid the planks upon the concrete, between and on all sides of the protruding bolts so that only an inch of thread showed. The tubular steel signal post — which had a square base-plate drilled to accept the four bolts — was struggled with until the base-plate was resting on the timber shuttering. The post was raised by the men to an angle of about 30 degrees and supported in that position by the wooden, 'out of use' box cover which would enshroud the colour-light signal head until it was required for use. The top platform and guard rails were bolted on and preparations were made for the final lift. Their length of rope was wrapped around the base of the post and tied to two pieces of point rodding set in the concrete. This was to prevent the base-plate moving out of position during the struggles of raising the signal. The hired ladder was then placed under the top platform and with a concerted heave the five men shoved the new signal up to about 70 degrees. At this the bottom rope prevented further movement so they slackened it and the post was given a final push to the perpendicular. They then rocked the assembly onto each edge of the base-plate in turn to free the shuttering beneath and thus to lower it over the bolts without 'burring-over' the securing bolts' threads.

The foreman of the gang got busy with a folding rule and a battered template kneeling on the ballast to mark out a piece of steel while a member of his gang enlarged a hole in another bit of steel with the end of his file and yet others busied themselves with bits of signal. Looking down from the signal box window it looked as if Heath Robinson was erecting a gallows for me and my world. Just as the signal head was placed on the top platform a car arrived and from it stepped a man in a lounge suit. He ordered them and all portable bits of the signal down to Oxford North Junction.

'Damn,' said the foreman, 'just as we was getting interested.'

So they departed, carrying the signal head, leaving the signal looking like nothing so much as a 14-ft-tall bird-table.

Not wishing to hang around this gibbet, I left, soon after this, to take up a vacancy in 'Smiling Somerset'.

CHAPTER NINE

SOMERSET SIGNALMAN

Somerset was a different world. Susan took a job managing several rented properties owned by a Bath businessman. He lived in a late eighteenth-century Gothick folly called Midford Castle overlooking the precipitous Midford valley south of the city and we had a 'tied' cottage in what had been partly a stable and partly a Gothick chapel. The chapel had a tower with a stone staircase leading to a corridor giving access to all up-stairs rooms. The staircase and corridor were quite definitely haunted. It was a very beautiful place, built of Bath stone, surrounded by great trees, looking down into the deep, narrow valley through the parkland. The track bed of the Somerset & Dorset Railway skirted the park fence and it was easy to drive a car on to the grass-grown ballast. From that point the car could be driven to and through the mile-long Midford tunnel, which Susan and I did when we had friends to stay — an after-Sunday-lunch-adventure for us all. The tunnel was curved so after going in a short way, daylight was cut off and the total lack of light produced a feeling that was weirder than the ghost back at the old chapel. In 1929 the crew of a goods train had been overcome by the locomotive's exhaust in the tunnel and the train had run away down the hill to crash on the curve at the bottom, near Bath station. From the castle grounds, Ivo Peters, the great railway photographer, had recorded the wonderful pageant of the 'Slow & Dirty' (or 'Swift & Delightful') 0–4–4 tanks, the graceful 4–4–0 express engines from the Midland Railway, the LMS 'Black Fives' and the massive Bulleid 'Pacifics'. One way and another the entire area was vibrant with ghosts.

I drove 12 miles through hilly, Mendip, country, down winding village streets lined with medieval, stone houses and ancient pubs, places with rich-sounding names such as Hinton Charterhouse and Norton St Philip to reach Clink Road Junction on the northern edge of Frome. The signal box was a small, wooden building in a cutting close to the Clink road bridge. It stood on the up side of the line at the 114½ mile post, on the inside of a sharp curve where the meandering Wilts, Somerset & Weymouth Railway made a sudden detour south-westwards to pass through Frome. It was as if the navvies of 1850 were happily digging a straight cut south when they remembered that they had to go through the town so they swung the line sharply to the right for a mile before resuming their former, southerly heading. In 1933 the GWR opened a by-pass to connect each end of the detour, like putting a string across a bow. Clink Road Junction was at the northern end and two miles further on was Blatchbridge Junction. This new cut formed the final link in the Great Western's holiday route to the west and along it had stormed the 'Kings' and the 'Castles' on countless heavily laden expresses. Curiously, the sharply curved line into and out of Frome remained the main line while the by-pass was the avoiding line or — to the men — the 'back road'. The next signal box north of Clink Road was Fairwood Junction, three miles away on the edge of the Westbury complex of junctions.

When I arrived there in September 1973 the signalmen had, in most cases, worked on that part of the railway since before or during the Second World War. Others had started an equally long time ago but on the Southern Railway and had been working on the Somerset & Dorset Railway until it was shut and had then transferred to the Western Region of British Railways. All of them were country railwaymen: warm-hearted, hospitable and experienced in various aspects of railway work. The first man I met from this admirable crew was something over 6 ft tall. He was on duty in Clink Road box the day I first went there. He unfolded himself from the decrepit armchair with such enthusiasm that his head knocked the Tilly lamp hanging from the rafter. It swung sideways with a great clatter as he boomed 'How do!' and crushed my hand in his bony fist. He whipped out a packet of cigarettes while the lamp was still swinging. 'Have a smoke!' Everything was an exclamation. I did not smoke and refused, rather diffidently, as he towered above me, a gaunt frame of a man, smiling, fag packet extended. He thought I was modestly refusing to take away his stores. 'Goo-on, have one — "Tiny's" offering!' This was 'Tiny' Fred Wilkins and I knew at once that I was going to enjoy working Clink Road Junction.

'Tiny' had spent his working life on the railway at Frome since 1942 and had worked as a porter, carriage shunter and signalman. From him I first heard of 'mad bloody cockneys': the speed-fiend drivers and fireman of Old Oak Common. When 'Tiny' was at Blatchbridge Junction 'back in steam days' he occasionally had to stop a 'hard hitter' owing to the section ahead being occupied and when he could finally 'pull off' for the express he would go and lean on the window bar to enjoy the sound of a 'King' or a 'Castle' being thrashed away up the bank to Brewham by a 'cockney', indignant at having his head-long progress interrupted by a swedey, Somerset signalman. 'Mad bloody cockneys', 'Ocean Mail Specials' and the 'Cornish Riviera' were very much part of the legend of this line.

The other man with whom I learned was Ken Russell, a spry, slightly built man with a dry sense of humour not to everyone's taste although I enjoyed his company enormously. The smartly kept little signal box had eighteen levers and controlled a simple, double-track junction but it was an interesting job with 45/50 trains on the two day-shifts and slightly less on nights. The first thing to learn was the routine of bell-codes including the special 'route' codes which were quite complicated; learn how to work the frame to set up the routes in seconds flat because it was a fast-moving train service; learn the train service and how long it took for trains of varying classes to run from 'a' to 'b' and also what they did when they got to 'a' or 'b' as this had an effect on their running times.

To set the route into Frome took eleven lever movements because we had 'movable elbows' otherwise known as a 'switch diamond' in the up main to allow 50 mph running across the sharply curved junction. This was an addition to my experience, my latest signalling pet. First the 'elbows' had to be unbolted — shove levers 15 and 16 back into the row of levers, then pull over 19, 17, 18, 15 and 16 followed by signal levers 7.6.3 and 1. Speed in setting the route and in dismantling it afterwards was vital if delay was to be avoided to trains coming up from Blatchbridge. The object was to run everything and stop nothing and many a down train was 'nipped into Frome a bit tight in front of the up fast'. Readers might find this alarming but it must be read in the context of railway jargon. If the Clink Road signalman decided he could get a down train into Frome 'across the bows' of an up train yet without delaying that up train he 'refused the road' for the up train to Blatchbridge Junction so the signals at Blatchbridge remained at 'Danger' — two miles away. There was great satisfaction in making nice judgements, slamming the road back after the down train had passed over the junction and instantly 'giving the road' to the Blatchbridge signalman. He would then whip his signal levers over and the Clink Road man would go on to the phone: 'Did that up train get your distant all right?'

'Dropped it down his chimney,' would come the laconic reply, using the time-honoured and by then thoroughly obsolete phrase.

Learning the box with Ken Russell, I spent hours — days and nights — talking about railway work and railway people; Ken would be in the chair, with myself leaning against the train register desk or working the box. Ken reckoned, as Elwyn Richards had done, that the best signalmen were those who could work safely without benefit of safety devices. 'The best chap as ever we had here', he said, 'came from Ilfracombe, somewhere small down that way. He took on at Frome North but all our track circuiting and interlocking stumped 'ee in th' end and when he saw a vacancy down Crediton way he took it and went home.'

Believing that the Board of Trade/Ministry of Transport

insisted on complete interlocking of points and signals I disagreed. Ken was scornful. 'Even on the GW at Radstock you could have the gates open for road traffic and the boards off for a train. On the S&D at Chilcompton you could have the main line boards off with the cross-over reversed.'

'No, that can't have been,' I said, trying to remain respectful of an old-hand. 'It wouldn't have been allowed by the Board of Trade.'

'Never mind thic "Board of Trade", I know what I'm saying.' Ken was very sharp and used the Somerset 'thic' for 'this'. He went on: 'When the Western took over the S&D north of Templecombe, the signal works came under the Frome Signal & Telegraph Inspector and he told me he had sleepless nights till he'd put in track circuits in all the boxes to make up for the locking they didn't have. Them ol' bwoys on the "Darset" — they didn't hold wi' all thic Western equipment, 'twas all foreign to they. It was all made of plastic so's they couldn't polish it and it locked up their workings. There was talk of going on strike.'

'What? Over putting in proper locking!'

'Oh yes. Them down at Evercreech had been able to make movements that they couldn't do once the Western put in track circuits. Delays were caused and they maintained it was all a plot to run down the line — cause delays and upset the travelling public.'

Western Region men in the area of the Somerset & Dorset felt strong ties of affection for the line and its legend was well known on ex-GWR territory. There were eleven big 2–8–0 goods engines on the line, designed specially to cope with the terrific gradients and, naturally, they were all highly regarded by the staff as very effective, very special machines. Occasionally one would have to be driven 'light' to Evercreech Junction, there to be turned on the turntable. The telephone message from the originating station to Evercreech signal box was: 'That's the big girl coming to swing her arse.' The most famous of all S&D signalmen were Percy Savage and Harry Wiltshire who worked a lifetime in Midford signal box.

During the exceptionally severe winter of 1947 the line was closed by deep snow throughout its length but Harry and Percy went to work each day to clear their points, work the levers as a test according to the regulations and to polish all the equipment. They were being paid during the suspension of services and wanted to do something for their pay. The S&D was closed permanently after the last train on Sunday 6 March 1966, and on Saturday 5th, Harry and Percy did their turn with the Brasso and the Ronuk floor polish so that the box was as sparkling clean after the last train as it had ever been during the height of the service. Ken said, 'Them old bwoys 'ud stand on the platform wi' their hats in their hands bowing, as the "Pines" went through. That was their crack train, that train, that line meant everything to they.' I knew the feeling well.

Railways were always a family affair and never more so than on branch lines such as the one from Frome to Bristol through Mells, Radstock and Clutton. It passed through beautiful country, manned by the same men year after year, carrying the same people and the same traffic, apparently for ever. The men had the job at their fingertips, it became 'like clockwork', so familiar that not only did they modify the timetables to suit themselves but were even able to 'nobble' a magistrate when that personage was a well-known traveller on the line. One legend was that Evelyn Waugh's aunt was Chairwoman of Radstock Bench of Magistrates and was well known for her kind heart. A man waiting to appear before her in court could go round to her house an evening or two before the hearing and have an informal session with her in her kitchen when he could better explain his case. Before the Second World War there was a porter at Radstock who had been summonsed by the police to appear before the Radstock Bench on a charge of 'Riding without lights'. This was worth 7s 6d in fines, money that could be better spent in the White Hart across the road from the station. The porter therefore concocted a good tale, intending to take it round to the Chairwoman's kitchen but before he did, she arrived at the station to catch a train or fetch a parcel. They knew each other well enough by sight so it was easy enough for the porter to get into wily conversation with her — and let her know he was getting married soon, and how he was saving hard to give his wife a good life, and how he had to make do with wornout equipment. 'Just look at thic old lamp on my bike, f'instance, ma'am,' he said, craftily. 'Why, it's so dim it gives only enough light to show others I be comin', it don't give I no light and it be so dim that I can't even tell if it's alight when I'm riding.' The Chairwoman knew nothing about the impending court appearance of the porter but when he did appear before her she was so sympathetic that she not only discharged him but ordered that he be given a florin from the Poor Box.

The 5.30 a.m. Bristol to Mells goods train was worked by three guards, week and week about. Being regulars on the job they rented from the GWR the shooting and trapping rights on railway land at Mells. The game they caught they sold to a Bristol butcher and from their enterprise they made a goodly sum — with a little bit of help from their friends. The timetable required that the Radstock signal boxes open at 7 a.m. so that the 5.30 Bristol goods could be placed in a siding to allow the following passenger train and another from Frome to cross each other at Radstock, the line being a single track with crossing loops at stations. But, for a consideration, the signalmen at Radstock would open early and the engine driver would go a bit faster so that the guard could reach Mells without stopping at Radstock. This gave him time to take rabbits from snares and set fresh traps before starting the work — shunting the yard and going to the quarry to fetch loaded stone wagons. The official programme then required the train to return to Radstock and shunt there until about 10.45 a.m. when a Radstock guard, fresh on, took over, allowing the Bristol guard to work back to Bristol in charge of a passenger train.

What actually happened was slightly different. Mells Road is at the summit of a steep incline, 1 in 48 rising from Frome and 1 in 68 falling to Radstock three miles away. The guard took his train to the Stop Board at the summit, pinned down sufficient wagon brakes to enable the engine to control the train on the down grade — and waved it good-bye. He then went back to shooting rabbits. When the train arrived at Radstock the fresh guard was waiting and the shunting began and continued until it was time to go, engine and van, back to Mells to pick up the Bristol guard and his haul of rabbits and pheasants. Back once more at Radstock the dead-stock was loaded into the Frome-Bristol passenger train and off it went, with the enterprising guard, all stations to Bristol.

Ken Russell had begun his career in the area around 1936 and had an apparently inexhaustible supply of stories, many of them giving a new slant to the famous phrase 'permissive society'. 'What about the Managers?' I asked, wondering whether to believe the tale. 'Didn't they ever come round to check on you all and what would they have done if they'd caught you?'

'Them days,' said Ken, 'the bosses didn't go around looking for trouble — not like some o' them we've got at Bristol now,' he added, in a tone of disgust.

'Are they a miserable crowd then?' I asked, somewhat alarmed, knowing that I would shortly have to go on the rules exam at Bristol.

'Some of them are useless. Wait till you meet the bloke we call "Tatty". Knows nothing and goes around making everyone's life a misery. He couldn't hold a candle to men like the old Superintendent, Reggie Pole, or his assistant, Soole. I think you'll find ol' Soole was a real enthusiast for steam engines even though he was assistant Superintendent. I don't think "Tatty" is interested in anything but finding fault with men.'

'But what would happen if you had been caught out one day?' I persisted.

'Well, they'd have more manliness than this lot, a better understanding. You'd get your written reprimand or whatever but at least you'd feel it was justified, that you'd been fairly dealt with. They were gentlemen. One day Soole comes to Radstock and finds one o' the porters cutting the station master's hair and a couple of townspeople waiting their turn. Soole was half-way through the door, sees the station boss under the white sheet and says, "Oh, I shouldn't be here." Five minutes later he comes back, everyone is off on the job in hand and the station boss is working in his office hiding a half-cut head of hair under his cap.' Ken and I laughed. 'The difference is', Ken continued, 'that nowadays, if "Tatty" was to come across that situation you'd have to go to Bristol — the full rigmarole — with "Tatty" pleased as punch at having shown what an eager-beaver he is. Another time Soole was down at Radstock for an LDC meeting*. After they'd dealt with everything Soole takes them all over to the White Hart for a drink. I can't see "Tatty" offering to do that and even if he did no one would want to drink with him. Anyhow, Soole buys a round and then gets on about how they could speed up the working of freight across the branch. "You'd have a job speeding up the 3.35 Marsh Junction," one of the ol' bwoys says, "they go through our place like lightning." Soole buys this chap another pint, gives him a nice smile and says, "How many times d'you reckon the Marsh Junction has been speeding past your box?" ' Ken chuckled. 'The crafty devil. There's ways and ways of managing men and Soole did most of his over a pint.'

So we ranged far and wide, setting the world to rights politically as we got to know each other better but always turning to railways and some outrageous tales — like the time that the Clutton and Hallatrow signalmen challenged the men in Radstock North and South boxes to a darts match at the White Hart. They were all on duty at the time but at a late evening slack period the Clutton man took the Permanent-Way Department trolley 1½ miles to Hallatrow, collected his mate and together they pushed and rolled the trolley 2 miles to Radstock. They had their game and a pint and set off home but became derailed, the trolley and one man went down the embankment and a badly sprained ankle was the result. They had to leave the trolley and hobble back to base. The last train of the night ran late that evening because the signalman was

* The local Trade Union/Management discussion.

not on duty to get the token out for it. Ken, from his armchair, could interrupt some tale such as that to check me as I was about to 'give the road' for a stone train from Frome, with a 'Don't give that the road, haven't you got a fast to come up the back road?' and then sweep on with his story. One morning during my second week there, he was telling me about the time Oswald Moseley came to Radstock before the Second World War. He was holding an open-air meeting before the towns-people and many coalminers were there. Moseley went off into his brazen-voiced rant and after a while asked, rhetorically, for support for his policies. A coalminer gave him a distinctly unrhetorical reply; jumping onto the platform he shouted, 'No, we won't — but I'll give you this.' He hit him so hard that, big man though Moseley was, he fell off the stage.

At that point in the story two figures in railway inspectors' blue suits slipped quickly past the rear of the box; I glimpsed them briefly through the small, back window as they hurried down the steep path, into the cutting. 'We've got company, Ken,' I said.

'Look out then, 'cos that'll be "Tatty" and his mate.'

The door crashed open and the two men came hurrying up the stairs. It was more like a police raid that a 'box visit' by the local, friendly District Inspector. I noticed that both men's hats seemed to be several sizes too big. Curt nods and brief greet-ings were the order of the day with many a searching glance into corners and into our lockers until Ken closed them. One ran his finger down the columns of the train register hoping to find uncompleted entries. They watched me work the box for a while, made an appointment for me to see them for a rules exam the following week and then left, their busy feet clatter-ing down the iron-shod stairs.

'They were a happy pair,' I observed. 'Are they all like that at Bristol these days. It never used to be like that.'

'No, luckily it isn't,' replied Ken. 'It's just that we see more of them than the others.'

'Hmm,' I mused, 'I don't fancy going up on the rules in front of a mean-looking pair like them.'

'I shouldn't worry about it,' replied Ken cheerfully, 'they don't know any more about the rules than you do — less probably. I'd like to have seen them up against ol' Jefferies at Radstock, he'd have sorted them out.' Ken was off again into recollections of a happier railway. Mr Jefferies had been a signalman at Radstock in the 1930s and '40s, Branch Secretary of the NUR, on the committee of the local Co-operative Society, a good organiser and a staunch communist. He protected all his members from over-weening authority. 'No one bullied us, but him,' laughed Ken. 'He had the first chance at any overtime that was going and generally ruled the roost like a feudal baron — a real, old-fashioned communist. He never stood for the National Anthem nor for anything else that people would stand for and he never took his cap off to anyone. One day he said to ol' Soole, "You and me, we're the same — you just get paid more than I do." '

The following week, as arranged, I went for my rules examination. I knocked on the office door and a deep, sonorous voice said, 'Come.' I went in and was surprised to find only 'Tatty' and his mate. One of them must have been practising The Voice. They were sitting, facing each other across a long table in a room of milk-coloured plywood with wire-reinforced glass in the windows. There was nothing to show it was a railway office except, perhaps, for their large, uniform hats hanging on the utility hat-stand and there was no decoration unless the posters counted as adornment and it is conceivable that a certain sort of person might have enjoyed them — they showed in colourful detail several types of heavy boot including some with steel toe-caps. I had plenty of time to take all this in because after uttering 'Come' not a word was spoken, both men appeared to be engrossed in important State papers. I was just becoming irritated and wondering if I ought to speak when 'Tatty' looked up, took off his glasses and stared at me. The lenses of his spectacles had the happy property of making his close-set eyes seem further apart than they actually were and as the spectacles were removed the eyes seemed to sidle in close together, the better to confer on what they saw. Right on cue his henchman spoke.

'Who are you?' He had well-greased, obedient, *disciplined* hair which seemed to be straining at the roots to sweep ever more obediently away from his forehead. 'Tatty' continued to stare, holding his glasses by one earpiece in what he obviously thought was an extra-intelligent, especially quizzing look. These were the men who had visited me at Clink Road only the previous week. I had to reintroduce myself and state my business whereupon 'Tatty' relaxed his quizzical stare, slapped his spectacles back on his nose — whereupon his eyes appeared to leap to attention — and cried, 'Oh! I thought you were a guard!' He roared with laughter while his henchman gazed at him admiringly. My attention wandered over to their hats while they got the last giggle out of their joke. Each hat had a huge badge made of felt and gold wire and I wondered if the intense pressures of their highly responsible office had compressed their brains to the size and consistency of a felt and wire badge. I was still dreaming when 'Tatty' said, 'No, no, old son — just our bit of fun — you go along with Eric here and . . .' He got no further, for the door was flung open and another Inspector burst in.

Without waiting a moment he butted in, addressing himself to 'Tatty': 'Hello, Pat — what d'you think? I've been given a waistcoat that's too small for me.' In the face of this startling news the rules and regulations examination was forgotten.

'Oh no, that's not good enough, Ian,' crooned 'Tatty', 'let me phone the Stores and sort it out for you.'

'Please don't trouble yourself, Pat, I'm sure you're busy with this bloke here,' he nodded in my direction and, with a quick wave, said to the other Inspector, 'Hello, Eric.'

'No trouble at all, Ian,' said 'Tatty', 'I'll phone them right away.' He picked up the telephone with a special flourish which showed off his white cuffs and imitation-gold watch strap. I sighed and stared at the images of steel toe-capped boots.

'Please don't trouble yourself, Pat,' said Ian. 'You're too kind.'

'All right then, I won't,' said 'Tatty', replacing the phone, glad to have shown off his cuffs and then, remembering the job in hand, he said, 'Oh — *sorry*, laddie [first it had been 'old son', now it was 'laddie'; I was thirty-two], go away with Eric. Eric, make sure you put him through his paces.'

With that we were dismissed and 'Tatty' turned back to Ian to pick up their conversation.

A rules examination with Eric could not take long and within the hour we were back in 'Tatty's' office. Eric told him I would 'do' so 'Tatty' signed my Certificate of Competence. Having completed that formality he came round the table and put his face very close to mine. I thought he was going to kiss me for one terrifying moment, then he said, very quietly, 'Now you're in charge of a signal box here — watch your step. I've heard things about you I don't believe but, all the same, I shall be watching you.' Speechless with embarrassment and confusion I felt my face going bright red. After a few seconds he spoke again. 'If an Inspector had said to me what I have just said to you I would be telling him who he ought to be watching rather than watching me.' His words burned their way like acid into my memory. I stared at the steel toe-capped boots and wondered if I was not dreaming and 'Tatty', getting no reply, told me I could go.

I was now a signalman at Clink Road Junction, my seventh signal box in thirteen years on the railway.

CHAPTER TEN

BROKEN RAIL

There was one small but vital fact concerning Clink Road Junction that I had not learned by the time I took over my shift. I learned the hard way. Clink Road and Blatchbridge boxes were switched out of circuit on Saturday evenings after the last train from Frome had passed. The Saturday late-turn man locked the box with his own key and brought it back with him at 6 a.m. on Monday when he came to re-open the box.

One cold, grey morning, just as dawn was breaking, I walked down the cutting-side path to open the box and it was only as I put my hand in my pocket, standing in front of the door, that I realised that the big old key was lying on the kitchen table at home. That sudden, sick feeling shot through my stomach. If I drove home to fetch the key the box would be an hour late opening with that much delay to the passenger trains. Down in the cutting the silence was mocking, the dull, steel rails curved away unhelpfully in three directions and the stone arch of the bridge was like a huge, laughing mouth as I looked up and down wondering what the *hell* to do. I shook the handle of the locked door in desperation — and then, aha! Above me was a window which had no safety-catch. All I had to do was to get up there, slide it back and I would be out of my difficulty.

I got on to the inch-thick wall of the concrete coal bunker, reached up, gripped the steel bar which went in front of each window and pulled myself up. As my knee landed on the window sill I remembered that the screw-bolt holding the bar to the front corner post was in rotten wood. My eyes focused on the bolt-head just in time to see it drawing slowly out. The bar fell away and I began to drop as if on a parachute. Time was suspended. I thought I was going to land on my back across the coal-bunker wall — my back broken. I landed, sitting, on top of the narrow wall of the coal bin. The pain was heart-stopping. I fell over sideways and grovelled on the grit path, almost unable to breathe. Gradually the pain subsided, my eyes opened and I lay on my side gingerly flexing my legs to see if anything was broken. My eyes were an inch above the gravel, looking below the wooden platform in front of the door — and there lay the box spare key. I was still walking like an arthritic jockey eight hours later when 'Tiny' Fred relieved me. 'What's up wi' thee, then?' he asked, ever cheerful. 'Got piles?'

'Something like that,' I grinned ruefully but I never did say what had happened — until now — I felt too foolish.

With men like 'Tiny' Fred, Ken Russell and Tom Baber to talk to I could imagine I was still on the steam-hauled railway, the 'family' feeling was strong and, paradoxically, I began to photograph diesels. 'Tiny' had worked Brewham box at the summit of a hard climb for east- and west-bound trains. Many east-bound goods trains took 'rear-end assistance' from Castle Cary, usually in the form of a pannier tank from Yeovil shed. At Brewham the banker was crossed to the down line and went back to Castle Cary or reversed into a short spur until there was a convenient 'path' down the hill. The engine of a Yeovil to Castle Cary 'pick-up' goods did a stint as banker before setting out for Somerton and Durston with an 'all stations' freight. At Durston it shunted trucks, exchanged traffic before reforming its train to return to Yeovil via Montacute along the old Bristol & Exeter Railway route. 'Tiny', like me, was fascinated by the intricacies of such matters as well as by the beauty of sight and sound of the steam-hauled railway; the intricacies were part of its beauty.

He once told me, 'The ten happiest years of my life were spent working "Blatch", steam days. There used to be a 10.17 p.m. Paddington to Plymouth parcels that ran down in front of the "Papers" — 12.15 a.m. Paddington to Penzance. The 10.17 used to go into the down loop at Athelney to let the "Papers" pass and then it [the parcels] would follow the fast into the same platform at Taunton so's they could transfer the Taunton-Exeter "shorts" from the fast to the parcels. The 12.15 was then "Right Away" to Exeter and the parcels would follow, calling at the small stations. Well, one evening thic parcels came down so early that Clink Road put it into Frome and I held it at Blatchbridge until the 12.15 Padd had gone by. I knew the chaps on the parcels didn't like being held back 'cos they didn't come to the box to make their tea. Well, I pulled off for they behind the fast, they could follow it all the way to Taunton, and I was writing in the register when that engine started. Wham! Wham! Wham! Gor — I was at the window like a shot. I'd never heard anything like it. Them mad bloody cockneys was out to show me a thing or two. They came blazing away over the junction and then I saw they had a "King".' His face was full of the enthusiasm he felt. 'I leant out of the window and listened to they all the way up to Brewham summit, you could hear 'em pasting that engine all the way — wonderful!'

Diesels in considerable variety passed Clink Road box in 1973. There were the 'Westerns' and an occasional 'Hymek', the Southern '33' and the Midland '45s', the little '31s' and the common old Class '47s' — very occasionally we would see a Class '37' from South Wales or a pair of '25s' coupled together, they were not much use singly. I became quite interested in photographing them. On an outing to the new Whatley Quarry railway, built by ARC Ltd, I met and became firm friends with that most artistic of the great railway photographers, Ivo Peters. Sitting above a tunnel mouth, waiting for a 'Western' we knew was up at the quarry to come back over the viaduct below us, we agreed that, while it was something of a come-down to be photographing diesels, at the same time they *were* forming the railway and we ought to be glad that there was still a railway to photograph. Clink Road box, close to the bridge, had several 'ians', people who spent hours leaning over the parapet, photographing and taking numbers. I remember especially the crowd that gathered for the first day of the new numbering system, when diesels carried their class number combined with a 'running' number hence D1657 became '47293 (or whatever). The 'Western' class diesels, peculiar to Western Region, did not receive this treatment because they had cast aluminium numberplates which could not be cheaply replaced in favour of painted-on numerals. In 1948, when the private railway companies were nationalised, the engines of the four companies were allocated blocks of numbers by Region — thus all ex-Southern Railway engines were in the 30,000–35,000 range — but GWR engines, numbered from 5 to 9091, had to keep their numbers because they were shown on cast-brass or cast-iron numberplates.

Express trains coming uphill towards Clink Road box off the avoiding line were running at 80–90 mph with an invisible bow wave of air before them which hit the little, wooden signal box with a wallop that made the windows shake as the train hurtled past. Trains coming uphill out of Frome were always labouring on the sharply curved, 1 in 130 gradient. I vividly recall one autumn evening after a warm day. I received 'Train entering Section' at 9.40 p.m. from Frome North for a train of stone. At 10 p.m., when I was relieved, I was still waiting for it and at 10.10 p.m. I stood on the path up the cutting side and watched as a 2700-hp 'Western' came inching up the hill, engine bellowing, wheels ringed with fire like Catherine-wheels in the dark. The diesel was so powerful yet so much at the mercy of the evening dew.

In season, Clink Road signal box was opened on Sunday to enable holiday trains to pass at close 'headways'. People came from Birmingham and Bournemouth to photograph and on fine Sundays there would be a party of local children sitting fairly quietly on the cutting side opposite the box, watching the trains and listening to the signal bells through the open windows of the box. Susan came with me on my 9 a.m. to 9 p.m. Sunday shifts. We brought pots, pans and the raw ingredients so that she could make a roast dinner and a cooked tea in the box. We ate as if in our summer house — only it was better than that, with the ringing of the bells, thumping levers and racing trains. Those must have been among the most successful meals she ever cooked.

The trains were a great, free show. They came from all the usual places such as Paddington, Plymouth, Penzance, Paignton, Weymouth, Cardiff and Bristol but also from North Camp (on the Reading-Guildford line) to Truro, Kensington to St Austell ('Motor-Rail'), Cheltenham, Dover and Moreton-in-the-Marsh. It was difficult to tell one from the other except for the route code on the front of the engine but at least I knew they were of the most diverse origins and that made all the difference — I could write the unusual titles in the train register. They were belled to me with route code. Trains which had to go into Frome had 1–2 beats added to the 'Is Line Clear?' code, thus the 9.30 a.m. Westbury to Weymouth passenger trains was a '3–1' but I got the bell as '3–1–1–2'. A train going to Weymouth via the Frome avoiding line, such as the 8.10 a.m. Cheltenham — normally a '4 bells' — was sent to me as '4–3–4' and I signalled it on as a '4–1–2' signifying it was for Weymouth. The junction for Weymouth was Castle Cary so the signalman there understood the message and signalled it on to Yeovil (on the Weymouth branch) as a plain '4 bells'. An express for Taunton via the avoiding line came to me as a '4–3–4' but I signalled it on as a plain '4 bells'. There were similar arrangements for up trains. Such intricacies might not be to everyone's taste but we all enjoyed them and indeed, they were in use at the instigation of one of the local, young, keen signalmen, John Francis.

The signalmen were 'free spirits', proud of their independence, but who at the same time tried hard to run the express trains, stopping trains and freights through the complications of the Witham, Frome and Westbury junctions without causing delay. All we required was to be left alone or receive occasional visits from some senior, respected supervisor. 'Tatty' was a nuisance but being stationed at Bristol he was too far away to bother us overmuch. One morning, however, a bombshell arrived in Clink Road box in the form of a young Manager from near-by Westbury. I was on duty and he delivered to me what must have been a specially prepared speech. I had never seen him before and he introduced himself thus: 'I am Mr Smith. Area Manager's assistant. You will obey me in all things . . .'

I recally only the opening line because after that I was projected into a state of some confusion and was still wrestling with the word 'obey' when he marched out of the box. Recovering, I rang Tom Baber round at Frome North. 'Watch out — your new boss is on his way.'

'What d'yer mean?'

'Wait and see!' I hung up so as not to spoil his surprise.

Twenty minutes later Tom was phoning me, his cidery old voice shaking with emotion. 'Did you have thic young lad wi' you just now?'

'Did he give you his speech?' I asked, laughing.

'Aha! That he did,' Tom's voice was shaking with anger in contrast to his usual cheerful, easy-going manner. 'I bin' on thic railway more'n twice as long as he's bin alive and I don't think I've ever been spoken to like that.'

'What do you reckon then, Tom?'

'I told him — you might be in charge, mister, an' I don't care whether you be or you bain't but you ain't a-going to talk to me like that so you can just get off out of here until you learns some manners!'

'Oh Tom!' I laughed, 'did he go?'

'He damn well had to — I chucked'n out!'

About a fortnight later a train of stone was derailed at Frome North owing to the worn state of the track. Tom was on duty. He telephoned the Area Manager's office at Westbury. 'Where's that clever young man as is in charge? We'm off the road down yere and I wants to know what I should do!' And not a wheel turned until the new young Master arrived and, somewhat hesitantly, got matters organised. He learned from fine men like Tom and very soon turned into a humane, useful colleague.

One morning I arrived for work at Clink Road and was informed by the nightshift man, 'We had a suicide during the night. Someone stepped in front of an up fast about three o'clock. The police are still down there trying to piece him together so you'll have to stop the down trains and tell them to look out for the cops on the line. Blatch is stopping the up trains.'

Round about breakfast time I had a sandwich in my hand when a constable came into the box. 'Right, that's it then, job over. We've put one man together, no one else involved.' He was carrying a clear, plastic bag. At first its contents did not register, then I saw what was in it — two human ears.

I made one forgetful mistake in the year I worked Clink Road box. This would have had serious consequences but for the vigilance of others and, had it reached 'Tatty's' eager ears, would have enabled him to create much work for himself from which he would have derived great pleasure. I was saved by the 'family' atmosphere of the railway.

I had with me in the signal box an unofficial visitor, a young man who worked for Western Region's Signal & Telegraph Department at Gloucester. He was making a pilgrimage to see what was left of the old railway. He was dressed in heavy, 'county' clothes — highly polished brogue leather shoes, cavalry twill trousers, a twill shirt and a tweed jacket with leather patches on the elbows. He seemed a decent sort, keen on semaphore signalling and an hour slipped by in 'talking shop'. I told him the story of the Kingham 'slip coach'. In 1970 a train-load of football fans was returning from Wolverhampton to Oxford and the rowdies on board became a nuisance. The guard, with the assistance of the two railway policemen on board, herded them all in to the rear coach, locked them in and then pulled the communication cord to stop the train at Kingham. The rear coach was uncoupled, protective detonators were placed a mile to the rear and the signal boxes on each side were warned as to what had been done. The rowdies were eventually removed in police vans and the guard received a good deal of well-merited praise from just about everyone.

The story intrigued my guest who revealed that he was a Special Constable who often rode on trains in that capacity to keep order. At this point one of the permanent-way men came into the box to say that there was a broken rail in the up main between me and Fairwood Junction and no trains were to go up until further notice until they had the rail replaced. I have to confess that the message went in one ear and out the other, the man returned to the site and my tweedy visitor continued his tale. He told me he was riding on a train in civilian clothes when he came across a youth writing in felt-tip pen on the end wall of the corridor. Brimming over with public spirit, it appeared, he had made a run at the boy, kicked him in the back — 'with these very shoes I've got on now' — and laid him low. I felt furious and at that moment a 'light' engine was belled as passing Frome. Fuming, I got the road from Fairwood, pulled my signals and then peremptorily ordered the 'public-spirited' gent out of the signal box. He was the only person to have suffered this fate but it was all he deserved.

The engine, a Southern '33', shot past as he made his stunned exit. Shaking a little myself, I sent it 'Entering Section' to Fairwood, gave 'Train out' to Frome — and then remembered what I had been told. I slammed the signal lever back a second too late, the engine had gone by. Five minutes later the same permanent-way man came into sight, running. 'Hey! We've got a rail out up there. Had you forgotten?'

'Yes, I'm very sorry — in one ear and out the other, I'm afraid, I'll put a collar on that signal lever now.'

He relaxed. 'Oh well, that'll be OK then. I stopped that engine. The driver'll think the rail broke after you'd pulled off.'

Early in 1974 I started work on my book about Great Western architecture and on 18 March I went to Tilehurst and Taplow to photograph buildings at those stations. I travelled by express train from Bath to Didcot and from there on the 10.35 p.m. Oxford to Paddington diesel rail car. This dropped me at Tilehurst and went on its way. Fifteen minutes later I had my photograph and was wondering how best to continue the journey to Taplow when the 10.5 a.m. Oxford to Paddington parcels train arrived at the up relief line platform and stopped, the signal at the end of the platform being at 'Danger'. There were Oxford men in charge and I was soon standing in the cab of a Class '31' diesel.

'Do you know why we're waiting here?' asked the driver.

'The last one up was the 10.35 Oxford twenty minutes ago, it must be stopped at Scour's Lane.'

Scour's Lane was the next signal, about three-quarters of a mile away, out of sight around a slight bend lined with bushes. As the driver was telling his secondman to go to the signal post telephone and report the position of the train to the Panelman, our signal cleared to a single yellow. The driver began to blow the brakes off when around the corner, at least 250 yards away, but coming back slowly towards us, was the 10.35 Oxford. The driver and secondman were out of the cab in a flash and went running forwards towards the rail car with their arms raised in the 'Danger' signal. I was busy taking photographs. The guard of the passenger train was riding in the rear — now the leading — cab so he was able to put the brake on and no harm was done.

What had happened was that the Panelman at Reading had crossed a goods train from the West Curve to the Down Yard, the route taking the train across all four passenger-carrying lines. One wagon became derailed on the yard points but not foul of the running lines — something the signalman could have seen had he been working the layout from the old, Reading West Junction signal box. As far as the Panelman could tell from his console indications there was a derailment and the entire junction was trapped, set for the crossing movement. After twenty minutes he told the driver of the 10.35 Oxford to reverse to Tilehurst, de-train his passengers and tell them to take a bus to Reading — there was a bus stop about 200 yards east of Tilehurst station. He had no idea how long the delay was going to be so he thought this would be for the best. But he had overlooked the parcels train which was indicated on his console as standing at Tilehurst.

There were several portly matrons to be lowered to the ground from the rail car plus a group of passengers for Heathrow via the road motor coach shuttle from Reading.

These were the ones with the luggage. Out it all came, down onto the ballast. In the comradely manner of partners in misfortune they helped each other move the heavy cases from the track to the platform, passing us railwaymen with never a word or a glance, up over the footbridge and out of the station, traipsing along the Oxford Road like so many well-to-do refugees. Having dumped them the 10.35 Oxford crept back to its signal at Scour's Lane — and behold! It was cleared for the now empty passenger train to proceed. In due course we were given permission to proceed over the telephone by the Panelman and we drew slowly away, hardly daring to look in the direction of the erstwhile passengers — but we could feel the fury of their gaze through the sheet metal of the cab as they stood forlornly at the edge of the bus-less road. When I got to Taplow the teleprinter had disgorged a highly efficient print-out so that everyone was well informed of our latest piece of inefficiency. The porter tore the sheet off and gave it to me. I still have it. It reads:

> 10.35 Oxford left Reading at 12.22, that is 51 late.
> 09.45 Weston 12.08 from Reading, that is 31 late.
> 06.35 Penzance next at 12.20, which is 18 late followed by
> 10.25 Birmingham left Reading at 12.02 which is 5 late.
> This is all due to a wagon at West Junction landing up on Olde England shutting up the shop. End.

The teleprinter operator's feelings of disgust and frustration can be felt from the way he constructed his message. Our railway could run superbly well until some small thing went wrong and plunged a whole district into chaos.

No small thing was the storm which raged for a week at the start of September 1974. Days of torrential rain were followed by Force 10 winds during the night of 6th/7th. Just before dawn on the 7th I was woken by the roar of the wind through the great and ancient beech tree that grew outside the bedroom window. It was a bit too early to get out of bed but I reckoned I might need some extra time on the road so, with a groan, I crawled out and set off for a six o'clock start at Clink Road.

The road was littered with twigs and small branches as the crazy wind tried to uproot every living and dead tree. Between Woolverton and Beckington I could see the normally placid river Frome leaping along in a mad, grey-black torrent, foaming and piling branches against the arches of its eighteenth-century bridge. The wind was strong enough to rock the car and after a 12-mile drive it was a relief to get out of that thunderous half-light into the cheerful, fire-lit interior of the signal box, nestling peacefully in the deep shelter of its cutting.

At 7.30 a.m. a 'light' engine passed Fairwood Junction coming towards Clink Road. At 7.31 a.m. the 5.45 a.m. Weymouth to Bristol rail car passed me on the up line and at about the same time — unknown to a soul — a large elm tree fell to the wind and lay with its trunk blocking the up and its massive boughs blocking the down line. The driver of the 'light' engine, having seen the last of Fairwood's signals and with the first of my signals two miles ahead, glanced down at a newspaper on his console and therefore did not see the tree. This apparent lapse in his look-out was, in fact, a blessing. Had he seen the obstruction he would have stopped short; as it was he smashed through to the far side. The windscreen shattered, the front of the engine took a beating and some bits of glass or wood entered the driver's eyes but, realising immediately that the up Weymouth would be close, he drove on and was able to place three detonators on the up main line a mile from the tree. He got back onto his engine and went forward, holding a red light from the cab. The Weymouth's driver thus received plenty of warning and stopped well away from several tons of elm tree in his path.

When the 'light' engine came under the arch of the bridge at Clink Road my first reaction was, 'Well — I know we're hard up for engines but this is ridiculous.' A second later I realised that something very unpleasant had happened and sent 'Obstruction Danger' to Bernie Miles at Fairwood. The driver came into the box with a face almost as battered as the front of his diesel but he told me precisely what had happened. The up line was blocked by the rail car, which was safely at a stand, so

I asked Bernie to send me 'Obstruction Danger' to cover the up line — the 6 bells I had sent him covered only the down line. The next job was to advise Bristol Control. We needed an ambulance for the engine driver; we needed the Permanent-Way Department with some powerful chain-saws and we needed some impromptu alterations to the timetable. While I was on the phone the guard of the Weymouth arrived in the box.

It was agreed that the Weymouth should come back, 'wrong road' to Frome, de-train its passengers into buses to be provided and then return to Weymouth as the Bristol to Weymouth rail car which was stuck on the wrong side of the tree. The guard of the 5.45 a.m. Weymouth saw me padlock the clamp on No 19 points and on the telephone Tom Baber assured him that it would be safe for his train to run 'wrong road' back to Frome. The guard returned to his train and conducted it back to Frome station. The passengers were just trooping out into the station forecourt to get on the waiting bus when I got the message that the line was clear. This was just as well because there were at least two bus-loads of passengers and only one bus. Back they all came, on to the train standing, rattling, beneath Brunel's wooden station roof. The guard gave 'Right' and off they all went — towards Weymouth. The line between Frome North and Blatchbridge Junction was a single track worked by 'tokenless block', so once a train had been signalled through in a particular direction it had to go, right through, to operate the track circuits in order that the route in the opposite direction could be set up. Apparently there was no provision for a train wishing to reverse its direction half-way through the section as was the case with the train standing at Frome. The train went 1½ miles down to the main line at Blatchbridge, stopped quite clear of the Frome line, reversed and went back again. The passengers must have thought we were all barking mad.

CHAPTER ELEVEN

STEAM FLASHBACK

Trains of stone-carrying wagons, empty, thundered through the cutting at Clink, the steel tubs booming and shaking as a big diesel hustled them along at 45 mph. Loaded trains came uphill no less precipitously, stone dust flying, as their drivers 'ran 'em', sometimes in the full knowledge that they were out in front of a 'fast' and on a 'tight' margin. These stone trains, hauled either by a 'Western', 'Brush 47' or '45' class diesel were going to or coming from the Merehead quarry of Foster Yeomen Ltd. The quarry was situated off the Cranmore branch, itself the stub of the line which had once passed through the Mendips to connect the GWR at Witham with the GWR at Yatton. The track accommodation at Witham was barely sufficient to cope with the traffic which led to some intriguing situations as the Witham signalman manoeuvred to make the proverbial quart fit into a pint pot. (See Appendix 4.) Soon after arriving at Clink I realised that Witham was a very desirable residence for a signalman who enjoyed organising trains. A vacancy arose there and, one year after taking the job at Clink Road Junction, I moved to Witham.

Witham Friary is an ancient hamlet astride the stripling river Frome, snug in a remote vale, miles off even a 'B' road at the end of a corkscrew lane to nowhere. A great Cistercian abbey, built at Henry II's expense as part of his penance for causing the death of his Archbishop, Thomas à Becket, once stood in fields close to my up advanced starting signal. Much of its stone and at least one of its fireplaces had been used in local houses but of the abbey there was no trace above the green fields but a small chapel, an offshoot of the looted, monastic settlement, still stood and was in use at one end of the village street. At the other end of the street, past a row of dormer-windowed cottages and a muddy gateway where Jersey cows gathered to bawl for the 'fogger', stood the Seymour Arms, close by the railway bridge. The pub, with its ornate sign, would once have been the watering-hole for passengers and staff at the little station on the bridge but in 1974 there was no station and the landlord with his wife were wise to rely for their living on milk.

The Seymour Arms, probably an early nineteenth-century building, sat four square and solid at the roadside, at once a public house and a farmhouse with mucky cow-yard attached. Anyone fortunate enough to have entered would have been served a decent pint of beer or home-made cider by Elsie. Often she came to serve straight from the farmyard, the evidence of her work coating her wellingtons as she clumped along the flagstoned passageway to the bar. You wanted beer? There was the oak barrel. Cider? Here is the barrel and, stooping in her wellies and apron, she turned the tap and filled your glass. A few crates of bottled beer and some brown shelves for chocolate and cigarettes more or less completed the catering arrangements. The public bar was brownish and dim, the walls a nicotine-cream colour with a bright green bench along one side, a couple of wooden tables with hard chairs, usually unoccupied. Sometimes I saw a pair of ancient farm workers, old mates, drinking cider and playing dominoes at a table by the only window in the room.

The signal box stood on the downside of the line about 200 yards west of the hamlet, on higher ground. It was a tall, brick building in the GWR's rather severe style of the 1890s. A flight of external steps led from the lineside path to the door which opened into an internal porch and the operating floor. The down distant signal lever, No 67, was close by and the lever frame, instrument shelf and long glass-cased track diagram stretched away down the length of the room. When I turned up one Monday to start I found Tom Baber near the door, by the instrument shelf, with a piece of bread in his hand.

'Morning, Tom,' I said, 'you'll be able to eat that crust in peace now.'

'Eh? Oh, this ain't for me,' he said, 'I'm feeding my mouse or I was till you frightened him away.' Tom, who up till then had been only a friendly voice at the end of a telephone, was about fifty-three, becoming stout with sandy whiskers on a strong-looking face which matched his character. He could yarn away for hours about his life on the railway and in the countryside, speaking in a Somerset cider-soaked accent.

'Now that you'm yer, you can get on wi' it,' he said, throwing me the duster from off his shoulder and retiring to the table and chair at the west-end window. A bell rang and with a loud squeak the mouse fell from under the instrument shelf onto the floor and went scuttling away into a pile of newspapers.

'He'll kill hisself one day,' said Tom laconically, reaching for his tin of tobacco and Rizla papers. 'He gets up amongst the wires and gets a shock when a bell rings — he don't ever seem to learn.'

Leaning on the booking desk after registering the bell code I saw some rabbits playing out in the field and mentioned them to Tom.

'Yer — I know most o' them by sight. Can you see the one with the white patch on its fur? We'd have trapped they years ago, set a snare early and had rabbit pie when we got home. Ever had rook pie? We used to put a lump of bread down between the stock rail and the blade o' the points and when a rook came along he'd put his head down to get it out and — ' Tom clapped his hands together — 'we'd slam the points shut and have rook pie.'

'Ugh!' said I disgustedly, 'you're pulling my leg.'

'No I ain't,' protested Tom, ''tis all good food. Have you ever had hedgehog — '

'No,' I butted in, 'I've never had hedgehog pie.' Tom chuckled. ''Tis all good food, you had to make do wi' what you could get once upon a time — the only thing I've tried what I couldn't eat was badger.' He told me about the local, annual badger roast and so the hours of the shift passed.

The signal box stood on the valley side overlooking the river

Frome. Meadows full of buttercups lay all around, crossed by hedges, dotted with big ash and elm trees. The mellow brick of the hamlet lay to the right whilst opposite and to the left the land rose to a wooded horizon. Through this valley the railway rose, climbing south-westwards towards Brewham summit on a 1 in 112 gradient and the big diesels, 'in the collar' almost all the way from Westbury, attacked the final two miles of the bank, past Witham, with an angry roar and a plume of black smoke. The 'King' class steamers would have been truly majestic as they came past Witham on a West of England express at 60 mph. The Cranmore branch, 5¾ miles long, left the main line on a sharp curve to the west a few yards to the left of the signal box and went straight up the valley side on a 1 in 49 gradient for half a mile before turning left to wind and climb through the hills. In steam days I could have watched a '45' tanky storm the bank and could have marked its later progress by the plume of smoke through the trees. Witham's layout had a spaciousness and the signal box, standing back a little from the main line, gave the impression of a grandstand view.

In 1974 the most exciting sight for me was to see a train of stone for Botley, or Luton, weighing around 1500 tons, come hurtling down the hill. By day the speed was obvious, smoke off the brake-blocks, stone-dust flying; by night speed was less obvious but there was plenty of Catharine-wheels as cast-iron brake-blocks gripped spinning, steel-tyred wheels. When I was standing on the wooden boards of the footway, crossing the tracks from signal box to branch line, waiting to take the token off the driver, this performance was amply exciting. The driver had more faith in his brake than I had and if anything went wrong I was in the right place to learn about it promptly. But it was fun. There was a lot of the old 'dash' about the proceeding, the train would always come very smoothly round the curve and the token would be handed off with the studied nonchalance and cheerful, inconsequential greeting that goes with a job where men know they are working skilfully and well.

The token, in its hooped carrier, was carried to the signal box and restored to its instrument. The token system at Witham was unusual in so far as the Witham signalman had total control over the issue of tokens. I merely pressed the brass plunger to give myself an electrical release for a token and then told Eric Compton up at Merehead Quarry ground frame what train was coming to him. If he wanted to send a train to me he asked for a 'release'. Once a token had been removed from either machine they were both locked until that token was restored. Merehead Quarry was served by a triangular junction under the control of the man at the ground frame. Trains left the quarry on condition there was not a train waiting in the branch loop at Witham to go to the quarry. The empties took priority because the loop had to be kept clear — the trains of empties would come down from Westbury, three in succession with the 'fast' behind so the Witham signalman had to dispose quickly of the goods trains — one to loop, one to stand on the up main line and a third to reverse into the down sidings. Obviously, these solutions to the problems of keeping the main line clear depended entirely on whether there was a train signalled on the up main or whether the down sidings were already full of empty wagons. Sometimes we had to ask Clink Road to send one of our trains of empties through Frome to ease the pressure on our own layout when stone trains and express trains were running thick and fast, occasionally the whole thing ground to a halt. The permutations of circumstances affecting train working at Witham seemed to be endless — which is why the 37-lever signal box was such a challenging and entertaining place to work.

Tom gave advice on which train to 'run' and which to 'hold' all in the same breath as he used to describe the working at Sparkford station in 1938, the qualities he expected in a Victoria sponge (he was an expert sponge-cake maker) or the snobbery of a certain bishop he once knew. Through this expertise in railway work mixed with story-telling I soon got the hang of the basics of Witham box. One day I 'supposed' that the road from Brewham to Westbury was an undulating one. 'Oh no it isn't,' said Tom emphatically. 'You can forget that bit of a hump between Blatchbridge and Clink, they don't hardly notice that, it's downhill all the way to Westbury. Back in steam days a "light" engine stopped on the up road at Brewham box — ol' Sid Fleming was on duty there. "There's something I'd like to try," this driver says to Sid.

' "Oh, what's that then?" asks Sid.

' "I'd like to see how far I could go on one puff of steam from here."

'Well, Sid told all the chaps what was going on, the engine — a "Hall" it was — had a clear road to Westbury and off it went — one chuff out of its chimney. Well, the road is so much downhill they free-wheeled all the way to Fairwood and had to brake hard for the turn into Westbury,' Tom finished triumphantly from his window seat, looking out over the branch. 'Oh! Here's the Luton just coming down the hill, you can pull off for they right away — the Penzance isn't about.'

I 'asked the road' to Blatchbridge — 5 bells — pulled points 32, bolted them with 31, pulled signals 5,6,7 and 10 and hurried down the steps and over the footboards to collect the token from the driver. The massive bogie of a 'Western' went grinding over the rails a few inches from my toes. Back in the signal box I sent 'Train entering Section' — 2 beats — to Blatchbridge as I passed the bell and put the token into the instrument. Turning to look at the train I saw that its tail lamp was quarter of a mile up the line. 'Don't those diesels motor!' I said to Tom as I gave 'Train out of Section' to the ground frame. 'A thousand tons or more behind the engine and they run like a passenger train.'

'Well, they could run 'em steam days too,' replied Tom. 'I do recall a summer Saturday when Exmouth Junction shed was getting low on coal and we had a trainload for 'em stuck up at Westbury. Summer Saturdays down this way in the fifties there wasn't a path for all the passenger trains let alone for loco coal but it had to go. Exmouth Junction was the Southern's most important shed between Salisbury and Plymouth. Control asked the driver if he'd go, given the road, and he said he would provided it was an absolutely clear run — 'twudn't be difficult to run, it was stopping he were worried about — twenty-five twenty-tonners o' loco coal and no brake.' Tom gave a short laugh. 'Well, that was only a little "63" engine but it came down here, all against the collar, so fast that the following Birmingham to Paignton excursion only missed the distant at every other box. 'Course, there were more boxes open in them days but even so, it's uphill for ten miles from Westbury.' I wondered, then, what other signal boxes there had been in those days.

'A lot more than now!' said Tom. 'Woodlands, between Blatchbridge and here, Brewham next along, then Pinkwood, Bruton and Wyke before Castle Cary, five extra signal boxes compared to now.' I expressed more surprise, most gratifying to Tom who blew a cloud of tobacco smoke at the ceiling to express his satisfaction.

I felt I ought to 'know the road' better and made several journeys from Westbury to Weymouth. Travelling in the cab of a somewhat underpowered Class '31' diesel, to hear it struggling and to see those curves and gradients unrolling before me enabled me to appreciate the skill and physical endurance of the men who had worked steam engines over the line.

On 3 April 1975 I went down to Merehead Quarry on 1070 *Western Gauntlet* and the driver spent the entire trip talking about steam days. The old East Somerset Railway through the Mendips from Witham was sharply curved and steeply graded throughout and as we bored up the initial 1 in 49 with 2700 hp thundering away like Woden's hammer behind our backs, the driver spoke about the time when practically all the traffic on the line was handled by pannier tanks. 'The biggest engine allowed was a "63" but it was always the Frome "77s" or "37s" and the Bristol "45s" — small engines, big loads — that took good enginemanship.' The huge diesel heeled around the curve at the head of the incline — thirty-five empty tubs, 227 tons in tow, 247 with the brake van — and the driver all but closed the throttle as the grade eased and the line curved gently through the woods.

'You could get fantastic work out of a little tanky if you knew what you were at,' he went on. 'One of the jobs we had out of Westbury was an "all stations" to Bristol via Trowbridge with a "Hall". At Temple Meads we'd take the coaches out to Malago Vale, back on the shed for coal and water and then work another stopper back to Westbury. Well, this day I was cleaning the fire as we stood on the shed and saw that some of the brick arch had dropped onto the grate and it looked as if more was going to follow. So we went to the foreman, failed the engine and asked for another. All he had was a "37" tanky. Well, my mate and I didn't mind, a little "pannier" tank with five coaches was OK over that road, so up the station we went. The engine wasn't so long out of Swindon — nice black paint just starting to get a bit grimy — we'd be all right.

'They put us through the Middle Road, alongside some train standing at our platform. "Must be something running late," my mate says, pointing at this other train. We counted eleven coaches before we got to the front. They were all for us! When our guard comes up to give us the load and saw the engine, he cussed because he thought it was the Pilot still on the train and he'd be late away waiting for the train engine to arrive. When we told him we were the train engine he cussed some more.' My driver friend laughed, and, taking his eyes off the track for a moment, turned to me: 'I don't know what he was going on about, it was me that would be doing all the work.' We went over the main road bridge at Wanstrow and he, like a good teacher, carefully remembered to point out the site of Wanstrow station. Then he went on: 'We had a bunker full of Midland hard coal and my mate says, "Fill the box with that till you get only yellow smoke showing. It'll burn like paper once we get going." We left with a full glass of water and the needle on the mark. "Put the feed on," say my mate, "here we go." And did we ever?! He gave it the gun and by East Depot we had them on the trot with the signalman leaning out of his window to watch — signalmen always liked watching a fireman slaving away!' He grinned across at me. 'I was raising steam and sweat in equal parts but I was determined not to be beat. I had the one injector on all the time but that wasn't enough to maintain the boiler water level the way my mate was using steam and if I put the second injector on as well it knocked the clock back*. My mate was taking more steam out of the boiler than the fire was making but with a station every two or three miles I could put the second injector on at the stops and keep the boiler topped-up. We hammered that engine so's we lost only five minutes to Westbury with a double load on a schedule designed for an engine twice the size of ours.'

We pulled steadily uphill to the ground frame at Merehead Quarry Junction. The driver handed the token to Eric Compton and we swung right over the points from the Cranmore line to the eastern arm, opened in October 1973, of the triangular junction, down and round into the quarry. Dense woods had been ripped open to make the new line and white stone dust smothered the ground and remaining trees. My driver kept his eyes piercingly on the curving, falling track, fondling the brake handle, conning us into the berth. He gave the brake handle its last turn; I felt the entire weight of the train push up behind then all was still save for the sound of our diesel engine, clanking quietly. We waited for someone to come and hook us off our train.

'There was a lot of fun to be got out of steam engine work,' I ventured, to start him off again.

'Steam could be bloody hard graft and uncomfortable, too, at times but we did have a laugh and there was the challenge of the engine every time you went out. These things', he thumped his fist on the diesel's console, 'have made life a thousand times easier but they aren't much fun. When they go they're great, when they don't they're a damn nuisance.'

'What was the hardest job you had out of Westbury?' I asked, thinking of the Channel Islands potato trains.

'The Weymouth stoppers,' he said promptly. Just then a shunter banged on the cabside. The driver popped his head

---

* Reduced boiler pressure.

over the side. 'I've hooked you off,' shouted the man. Go over
there and I'll hook you onto 7609 set.' In a few minutes we
were coupled to forty-two sixteen-tonners loaded with stone
for some new road. This lot, weighing around 1500 tons,
Western Gauntlet would push uphill along the western arm of
the triangle to the Cranmore line — but first, tea, biscuits and
more talk. We sat in the cab surrounded by dusty trucks,
tracks and loading machinery, the forest rising high above.

'The stoppers were harder than the "Perpots" then?' I asked
using the railway's old telegraphic code-word for the seasonal
special trains of potatoes.

'Oh, the "Perpots" — no, at least with those you were on the
run non-stop. The Weymouth stoppers were all stop and start
on heavy gradients — eighteen stations in sixty miles to
Weymouth and the same back again. Drive you daft, starting
and stopping — and it used a hell of a lot of coal.'

'Which, of course, you had to shovel on,' I finished for him.
After tea and biscuits and a fag, we tidied the cab and set about
leaving. He gave a blast on the horn to call the guard, who
looked out from the brake van, gave 'Right Away' and we
were off. I stood in the doorway to get the benefit of the sound
of a 'Western' unleashed. The driver leant well outside with
one hand reaching inboard to the throttle handle. He gave it
one notch, two notches, the engine roared, howled and 1500
tons of stone and steel began to creep inexorably uphill. The
guard in his van, at what was temporarily the leading end of
the train, waved us on and at walking pace *Western Gauntlet*
rolled its cumbersome, unbraked train up to the Cranmore
'main line'. We were trundling into a dead-end siding with the
Cranmore line on the left, the driver was braking and I could
feel the train's brute weight dragging the 100-ton engine on
towards the invisible buffers. The driver must have had a fence
post or some other landmark to gauge his final brake for he
stopped the train with the engine just clear of the points out on
to the 'main line', the last few feet being covered by the weight
of the train dragging the brake-locked locomotive along the
rails.

We stopped at Quarry Junction ground frame as a 'Brush 47' came uphill towards us, its driver dangling the hooped token carrier over the cab-side. Eric went to collect it. From up there the true depth of the valley through which the real main line ran was apparent. We were 600 ft above sea-level, 350 ft above Witham, looking down on a wonderful panorama of woods and fields. The other train trundled past, the drivers exchanging waves. My mate had just finished a meticulous sharing of the remaining tea when Eric rapped on the cab-side with the token carrier. 'Right away, driver!' I took the token, handed it to the driver who laid it on his console and, releasing the brake, allowed the train to roll away downhill. The tea was getting rough-edged but the view was magnificent and even the smelly old diesel did not seem too bad in the company of such an excellent mate. I remarked on the essential contribution that tea has made to railway work and described a home-made immersion-heater I once saw a fireman using to boil the water in his tea can; he screwed a U-shaped piece of copper tube to the steam lance connection on the engine's smokebox, when steam passed through the tube it heated it and boiled the water. My driver friend thought this was clever but restricted to use when the engine was stationary. He went on:

'I was a fireman and me and my mate had to go out to Heywood Road Junction to relieve a "Broc" special — broccoli up from Penzance. The engine turned out to be a "County", good, strong engines if you can get them right but sods for steam if you haven't got the knack with them. Anyhow, we got on, they got off and my mate told me to put the tea can in the fire on the shovel to make a brew before we started. But just as I was pulling the shovel out of the fire I somehow managed to knock it against the side of the hole and the whole lot went up in a cloud of steam. Bloody wars! I knew my mate was annoyed but he didn't say anything — he just got that train rolling. I was making steam and sweat in equal parts and we went up the bank from Pewsey to Savernake like a blessed passenger train. He just about pasted me, letting the lever down little by little till we had sparks like cricket balls coming out of the chimney on the steepest bit by Burbage Wharf. Over the top, through Savernake station, he comes across to me with a wicked grin and says, "How would you like a cup of tea now?" '

We both laughed at that and he began to brake so as to stop at the head of the incline to allow the guard to get off and pin down wagon-brakes. 'You're laughing now,' I said, 'but did you laugh then?'

'Well, he was a good mate, we were always pulling each other's leg. It'd have been different if he always drove like that. A bad mate on a steam engine was just plain misery.'

The guard shouted 'Right Away' and with some throttle to get the train moving we set off down an incline which seemed to me to be as steep as a roller-coaster in a fairground with Witham box looking very small and faraway at the bottom. My driver was silent and I knew he was considering something. Finally he said, 'I've got a letter at home, thanking me for some good work from Reggie Hanks — he was General Manager a bit before your time, I should think. You'd have liked him, he was a great steam enthusiast.' I was able to surprise my driver by telling him that I used to live near Mr Hanks in Oxford and he had told me a lot about his footplate exploits — the only General Manager to regularly act as fireman on the train that took him to work, just the sort of Boss that all railwaymen were proud of. My mate agreed with this and went on: 'The chap I was firing to got a letter too. We relieved an "Ocean Liner Special" that had come into Westbury, I can't remember why now, they were usually non-stop Plymouth to Paddington. There must have been something serious wrong — anyhow — the train had been standing there for twenty minutes and as we left my mate said to me, "How about it then?" I said I didn't mind, we had only six coaches and we just about flew. Someone on the train must have written to Hanks about it because we got a letter thanking us for the effort. But even without that I'd remember that run for the speed and for the engine,' he paused for effect and added grandly: '*Isambard Kingdom Brunel.*'

He brought the engine to a stand on the footboards at Witham so I could get down on to a safe footing with the token and, very reluctantly, I left this excellent driver to carry the token up into the signal box.

CHAPTER TWELVE

SIGNALMAN'S NIGHTMARE

I took over my shift at Witham in September 1974 with the minimum of 'rules' fuss. 'Tatty' had been most concerned about the working of the Cranmore branch. 'What are the regulations governing the working of the Cranmore branch?' he asked severely. Under normal circumstances that was a very large question, like asking an aspiring cleric, 'What does it say in the Bible?' but circumstances were not normal and I was able to answer in a word: 'None.'

'What d'you mean: none?' he snapped, thinking he had scored a hole in one with me.

'Exactly what I say. The system of token working on the line is unknown to any rule-book I've ever seen and you haven't issued the signal box with any special instructions to cover it.' Confusion and disbelief fought for possession of his face. 'Go and have a look in your files,' I suggested.

'No need for that, just trying you out. Now then, what would you do if. . . ?

We went off into some standard questions on double-line work. The examination did not take long and shortly I was on my way home as signalman at Witham (Som.).

At ten minutes to six on the following Monday morning I walked along the path to the signal box. There was a sharp wind hissing through the dawn, through the wheels of the wagons left on the sidings from the previous day's engineering work and I was glad to get into the shelter of the box. Inside it was curiously silent. No Tom Baber, no fire. The levers seemed to be waiting for a duster-clad hand to throw them across their quadrants — action and some cheerful noise. I put my coat on the hook, my food-bag on the locker-top and telephoned Westbury South box to discover the traffic situation. The

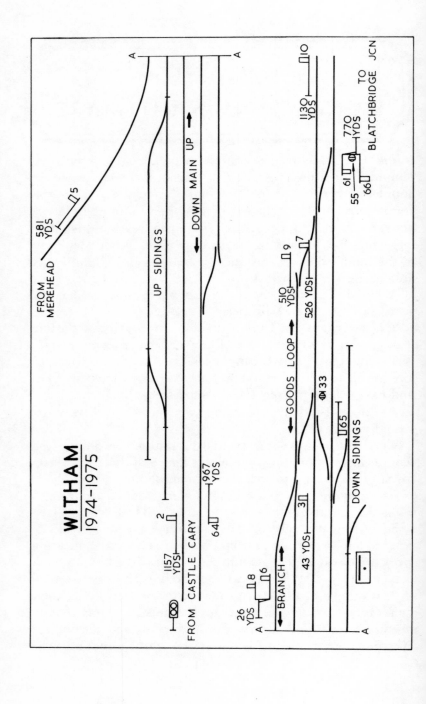

WITHAM
1974-1975

FROM MEREHEAD
581 YDS

FROM CASTLE CARY

UP SIDINGS

DOWN MAIN UP

1157 YDS

2

967 YDS

64

5

GOODS LOOP

510 YDS

526 YDS

9

7

33

65

3

43 YDS

26 YDS

8

6

BRANCH

DOWN SIDINGS

1130 YDS

10

770 YDS

61

55

66

TO BLATCHBRIDGE JCN

A

A

A

phone was cold and clammy. Tom Lamb answered, he was at
the end of his shift, waiting to be relieved by Bob Pritchard.

'Witham here, wanting to switch in. What's about, Tom?'

'There's nothing on the up but the Maiden Newton stock is
on the down road, it must be passing Clink Road now.'

'OK, I'll switch in now.' I put the up line signals back to
'Danger', pegged the down line instrument to 'Train on Line'
and turned the block switch brass handle from OUT to IN.
Then, having got the attention of Tom Lamb and Joe Apsey at
Castle Cary, I sent the 'Opening Signal Box' code — 5–5–5.
The high-toned and low-toned bells clanged out the acknow-
ledgement, the echoes awoke — Witham was in business. I
entered the fact of opening in the train register — the pages felt
cold and damp — put the kettle on and set about lighting the
stove.

The 5.55 a.m. Westbury to Maiden Newton empty diesel
rail-car rattled past out of the rising sun at 6.15 a.m. followed
by the 5.30 Westbury to Merehead empties. The 'Ganes'
(eight-wheel wagons), carrying old track sections from the
previous day's relaying job, were parked on the down siding
and had been parted so as not to block the foot crossing; I
walked between the big, oval buffers, carrying the token for
the branch train. There had been a certain amount of nonsense
over the Sunday job — relaying the up main line between
Witham and Blatchbridge — and Ron Kirby, the signalman
who had worked the box, left an explanatory note. The new
track sections had come up from Taunton on two trains and
one of the locomotives, a 'Brush 47', had failed on arrival and
was parked in the down sidings. The new track had been laid
but there had been some difficulty in hauling fresh ballast to
the site so the old ballast had been put back and an extra-severe
speed restriction was in force over that section. Last, but not
least, one of the 'Ganes' carrying the old track had a hot axle
bearing which would require attention before it could return
to Taunton. The 'cripple' was the last of the front part of the
train, immediately on the Taunton side of the foot crossing.

Eight minutes after the 5.30 Westbury had gone down the

branch a 'light' engine arrived from Westbury to collect the 'dead' diesel. Whoever had sent the engine had not known that the 'dead' engine was behind the long train of 'Ganes', shunting was required and as the engine had not come equipped with a guard or shunter it returned Westbury-wards at high speed. Various regular trains passed. At 8 a.m. I called the 'C&W' (Carriage & Wagon) Department to tell them about the crippled 'Gane' and at 9 a.m. an engine arrived from Westbury to haul the 'Ganes' to Taunton. The crippled wagon was shunted out of the train and finally placed in the siding in front of the 'dead' Class '47'. At ten o'clock, as a stone train was coming down the hill from Merehead and as two, Class '25', diesels coupled together were arriving at my home signal from Westbury, the '10 a.m. Witham to Taunton Fairwater' pulled out of the down siding, signalled '1–4' on the bell with the appropriate 'box to box' message. The leading '25' was for Cranmore, the trailing engine was to take the 'dead' '47' back to Westbury. I went out, fetched the token from the Merehead train, put it in to the machine and withdrew it again. The enginemen uncoupled their engines outside the home signal and when the stone train had gone I turned the first engine on to the branch loop, reversed the road and brought the other down to the box. As it was approaching I hurried out across the footboards with the token, back into the box to shunt the second engine to the down sidings and to give 'Train out of Section' for it to Blatchbridge. The bells and levers had been clashing and ringing enough to delight the heart of any railwayman since six o'clock and still the work went on, another stone empties from Blatchbridge as the men with the Class '25' shunted in the down sidings. They finally left for Westbury at 10.58, belled '1–4' with the 'box to box' message: '1 live, 1 dead for Westbury'.

The C&W men arrived in their yellow, Ford van at about this time, looked at the axle bearing and reckoned they'd need two hours to fix it. I telephoned Bristol Control to order an engine to work the solitary 'Gane' to Taunton at 1 p.m. and suggested that the spare brake van, left over from the two trains that had come from Taunton, could be worked home on the special. Two or three trains went by uneventfully but at 11.25 a.m. the Sheephouse Crossing telephone rang. Sheephouse was about a mile the Witham side of Bruton and was used frequently by a local farmer to move cattle across the line. He would first phone and ask permission but this would be early in the morning, it seemed late to be moving the cows so when I heard a female voice with an outrageously Somerset accent I naturally thought someone was pulling my leg. 'Ooo! Be that th' signalman? Ooo, hello m'dear — wa'al, ower ship be aal over the line down yer!'

Well, of course, I did not believe a word of it, replied in a similar voice and, excusing myself, went off to answer a bell. When I went back to the phone I asked in a normal voice, 'Are you still there?' quite believing that the Permanent-Way Patrolman or some other railwayman would now reveal himself. From the other end of the wire came the voice again. 'Ooo, hello m'dear. Whur's that nice young man I were talkin' to just thic minit?'

I rang Joe at Castle Cary and between us up and down trains were stopped and their drivers cautioned. Next I sent a call for assistance to the Permanent-Way Department at Westbury and lastly I phoned Bristol Control to tell them about this fresh cause of delay to trains. Between Woodborough and Bruton, about 30 miles, we had that morning four heavy delays for down trains and three for up trains.

The return train from Cranmore arrived at Witham at 12.30 p.m. with four tankers from the Shell depot. These were shunted into No 1 Up Siding in front of empty stone wagon set 7661. The Class '25' then brought the spare brake van across to the down siding. By the time the shunt had crossed from the branch to the down main, the engine had 'run round' the van and shoved it into the siding, it was one o'clock and the 8.35 a.m. Penzance was about to leave Castle Cary. As it would be starting from Castle Cary and as it would have to travel at 'Caution' over the steepest part of the bank I decided to let the Class '25' go before the fast. I told the driver the tale and gave him his chance. He took off like the proverbial 'bat out of hell'. As they roared away I gave Eric at Merehead Quarry ground frame the release for a token for the Merehead to Ipswich stone train and, at 1.15 p.m., as the 8.35 a.m. Penzance was hurrying by, the stone train arrived. More levers hastily slammed to and fro, down the stairs and across the tracks to collect the token, back into the box and restore the token to the instrument.

Sheephouse Crossing telephone rang. It was the Permanent-Way Inspector giving the 'all clear': 'Sheep all gone and fence mended'. I thanked him and rushed to pull the levers for the Cornish Riviera, hoping to give it a clear run. No such luck. It had already passed my distant at 'Caution', the driver saw all the stop signals lowered and came by blowing a sarcastic 'tut-tut-tut' on his horn, believing that I had been slow in pulling-off! Chris, at Blatchbridge, gave 'Train out' for the 8.35 Penzance. I promptly 'asked the road' for the Ipswich stone train and Chris 'asked the road' for the 9.48 a.m. Fawley to Tiverton Junction petrol train. The Fawley was creeping down to my home signal as the Cornish Riviera cleared Castle Cary. I lowered the down home and then 'got the road' for it from Castle Cary, lowering the other signals.

Behind the Fawley was a 'light' engine to work the 'Gane' to Taunton. The engine arrived, shunted into the down siding. I cleared the section and Chris promptly 'asked the road' — 3–1–1–2 — for the 12.5 p.m. Bristol to Weymouth rail-car. Moments later Joe Apsey 'asked the road' on the up line for the 12.15 p.m. Weymouth to Bristol. Following the 12.5 Bristol were the 11 a.m. Reading to Exeter goods, the Westbury to Yeovil parcels and a tamping machine for Taunton. I had my eye on the 12.30 p.m. Paddington, due in forty-five minutes, and asked for the tamping machine to be turned into Frome while I dealt with the other trains at Witham. The 12.5 Bristol cleared Castle Cary at 1.37 p.m., the Witham to Taunton special was ready so I turned it out onto the down main, signalled '1–4' with the 'box to box' message: '1.38 Witham to Taunton Fairwater'. It left, one 'Gane' and a brake van hauled by a Class '47' diesel, as the 12.15 Weymouth went by on the up line and as the 11 a.m. Reading was trundling down between Blatchbridge and me. The 11.55 a.m. Paignton whizzed past as the Reading was pulling slowly up to the box. It was normal for the train to be crossed to the up main to allow the 12.30 Paddington a clear run and the driver was leaning out, waiting for instructions. As I leant out of the window I could see my relief, Ron Reynolds, walking along the path. The 'Western' diesel grumbled down.

'Set back into the down siding,' I shouted to the driver who waved and revved-up.

The guard of the train was waving to say 'Train complete', his van was more than 440 yards ahead of the home signal. I could 'knock out' to Blatchbridge and accept the Westbury to Yeovil parcels, 1–3–1 on the bell. Seeing that I was enjoying myself, Ron went across to get the token from the stone train. The parcels would have to cross promptly to the up main so I did not see the route for the stone train to leave. The 12.30 Paddington was approaching Clink Road; at Blatchbridge the signals were at 'Danger'. I had about ninety seconds to give Chris Burden the road for the 'fast'. I set the electric motors running on the distant cross-over points and walloped the lever over the instant the indicator showed 'Point Reversed'. There was an answering 'honk' from the diesel and a plume of black smoke from a powerful acceleration which proved that the driver was aware of what was behind him. I leaned anxiously on the instrument shelf, hoping that the guard would be equally alert and wave 'Train complete'. He did. I reset the road, strode to the bell, tapped out '2–1' and turned the indicator from 'Train on Line' to 'Line Clear', rattling out the 4 beats without waiting to be asked. Chris, for his part, knew the score and was waiting on his levers at Blatchbridge. Thirty seconds later he sent 'On line' — 2 beats. In steam-age jargon, he had 'dropped his distant down its chimney'.

With the parcels train drawn down to ground signal 33, clear of the loop exit points, I set the route, 'got the road' and pulled off for the Ipswich. Ron put the token into the instrument and took his jacket off, ready to settle into the job. But first he had to get rid of me. By some people's standards I was trespassing! After the 12.30 Paddington had passed, I signalled the parcels back onto the down main. It left at 2.18, followed by the 11 a.m. Reading at 2.30; the tamping machine had just enough time to run from Blatchbridge to Castle Cary loop without delaying the 1.30 p.m. Paddington.

'Running 'em today, then, Adrian?' said Ron, with an understanding smile.

All the signalmen tried to run as many trains as possible. We kept in constant touch by phone not only to co-ordinate our plans but also to see how well — or badly — they worked out. We felt that we were experts, masters of the job, and enjoyed working without supervision; indeed, we did not need any supervision. That is not to say we did not have Supervisors, we did. They came in two categories: the humane, sensible types; and 'Tatty' sometimes accompanied by his Supervisor whom I shall call 'Sunshine'. As far as all the signalmen were concerned they came only to look for trouble, to show what eagle-eyed experts they were. In fifteen years I had never come across anything like them and nor had men with three times my service. Typically, on the one occasion when there was the coincidence of a minor emergency and 'Tatty's' presence in the area, 'Tatty' made a dash for home. Westbury Area Manager asked me and others concerned with this to write a report about it but none of us was there to complain about officious officials — they were there to bully us!

One afternoon, 'Tatty' walked into the 99-lever Westbury North box. It was 2.20 p.m. and the off-duty signalman was still in the box talking to the man who had relieved him. 'Tatty' put them both on a charge because they were breaking clause 'e' of Regulation 2 of 'Signalmen's General Instructions 1972'. So they were, as the stunned signalmen realised when they had a chance to think about it, but that did not lessen our sense of hurt at the Inspector's officiousness. A new signalman took over his shift at Heywood Road Junction on the eastern edge of the Westbury complex in 1975 and shortly afterwards was visited by 'Tatty' and 'Sunshine'. The latter seemed to all of us to be possessed of an inexplicable urge to brow-beat. He looked the new man up and down and asked, 'And what did you do before you came here?' His tone offended the man who looked him straight in the eyes and replied, 'I was in the Army — for the last two years in Belfast. Where were you?' Quite unabashed, 'Sunshine' replied, 'Then may we expect a little more discipline from you?' The new man left the job after a year, disgusted with the atmosphere which this official and others had created.

All this was a very far cry from the gentlemanly railway I had grown up with. Talking to men like Tom Baber or Ron Reynolds I could forget that people like 'Tatty' existed but the old-hands were retiring and by mid-1975 I was, at thirty-four, the oldest person on my shift between Westbury and Castle Cary. There was to be a panel signal box at Westbury, controlling the routes as far west as Somerton linking up there with the area controlled by a proposed panel at Exeter. There did not seem much point in staying; I discussed it with Susan and we agreed that the best course would be to leave and to try to make a way ahead as a writer on railway history.

In 1975, April had been warm, June was hot and July was sweltering. At 1 p.m., one day in July, my friend John, a signalman at Witham, left his lodgings at Trudoxhill and cycled through the lanes for a two o'clock start in the signal box. He had a bad headache and by 3 p.m. the pain had become so strong that he realised he must be ill and asked the Westbury Supervisor to send a reliefman. He continued to work the box because otherwise the freight trains would come to a standstill. He could have switched out but there was a train of empty petrol tanks from Tiverton Junction to Fawley which had to call at Witham to pick up and there were also stone trains and stone empties on the move, all of which would have been stymied without a man to work the points.

The Tiverton Junction petrol empties arrived on the up main when a stone train was approaching from Merehead. John reversed points 32 for the petrol empties to reverse off the up main but forgot to pull the other lever in the route, No 25, to divert the train from the branch line to the up sidings. Ground signal 33 could be lowered for any one of three directions so he was able to pull that lever and at that the train began to 'set back' — down the branch line. The stone train was coming down the 1 in 49 gradient at the time but its driver managed to stop. The Tiverton Junction stopped when its guard saw what was happening and the two trains ended up facing each other a few yards apart on the single track. Everyone was alert except John who was very ill. Several irate trainmen betook themselves at high speed to the signal box, intent on rebuking — if not actually strangling — the man who had given them such a bad fright. They found him unconscious on the floor and immediately their ire evaporated.

He was obviously sick so they phoned for an ambulance and made him as comfortable as they could. No harm had been done, the 'family' atmosphere saved the day and nothing more would have been heard of the incident had not John, full of a good man's contrition, reported himself to 'Sunshine'. John had had to go to hospital in Bristol and on his release, waiting for the train home on the station, he had gone to 'Tatty & Co' to confess his error. He must still have been in shock. He was the proverbial fly walking into the spider's parlour and, like spiders, they showed him no gentlemanly concern or pity for the circumstances he had found himself in. They booked him.

John was a jazz musician and in the interval between his confession and the day of the Inquiry he was offered a job with the Temperance 7, playing 1920s music on board *Queen Elizabeth 2* during a cruise to the Canary Islands. He had for some time been wondering whether life was worth living under the Bristol dictatorship so he leaped at the offer, handed in his notice to the Area Manager at Westbury and was away two weeks later. The Area Manager's organisation felt no obligation to tell 'them over at Bristol' what had happened so when John did not arrive for his Inquisition, 'Tatty' phoned Westbury to ask where his latest victim had got to. The clerk on the Westbury end of the line, knowing the whole story, savoured the moment and said, 'John? Where is he? Oo — let me see now. Well, the *QE 2* left Southampton about three days ago — I should think he's down around the Canary Islands by now.'

Staff shortages and staff holidays put us on twelve-hour shifts and I was on 'twelve-hour days' during the first week of August. The dawns were warm, the days scorching and the evenings sultry. On the night of 4/5 August a thunderstorm kept half Somerset awake and at 5.30 a.m. on the 5th I drove to work over steaming roads under beautiful, sunnny, cloudy skies. At work I discovered that the lightning had destroyed the new-fangled 'tokenless block' system of signalling on the single line between Salisbury and Exeter so that trains to and from Waterloo were expected to come through Witham. That was both interesting and acceptable — what was not all right was that our electric boiling ring had become thunderstruck and there would be no tea for that day.

The sun, having dried up all the clouds, blazed out of a bright blue sky; all the windows in the box were open and at midday the signal box thermometer was registering 90 degrees Fahrenheit. The Cornish Riviera went down on time but after twelve minutes had not cleared Castle Cary so I telephoned the newly appointed signalman to ask if he knew where the train was.

'Oh yes, I've got it standing here.'

'Why? What's the matter?'

'Well, that last up fast hit a sleeper that had been put on the line between Athelney and Somerton and Control says nothing can go down until the line has been examined.'

'That's a load of rubbish,' I said impatiently. 'Let the fast go. Somerton will send it through to Athelney to examine the line under Regulation 15; if they see a sleeper on the line they can just stop and take it off.'

'Oh, I couldn't do that,' said this young and inexperienced person. 'Control . . .'

'Stuff Control!' I snapped, full of frustration, thinking of the passengers on that crowded train, each with an expensive ticket in his or her pocket, all delayed because someone at Bristol did not know the rules. 'I'll go and sort Control out and we'll get that train on its way.'

I put the 'box to box' phone down and rang Control. I cannot write the precise words I used because they were 'heated', suffice it to say that I asked, 'What are you doing with the Cornish Riviera?'

'I am preparing to divert it via Yeovil and Exeter Central owing to the line being blocked at Athelney,' he replied very stiffly.

'But the line isn't blocked. There was a sleeper on the line, it's gone now. The 11.30 can go down and get through from Somerton to Athelney using Regulation 15 — "Examination of the Line".'

'I think you should mind your own business,' retorted the voice.

'It is my business,' I snapped back. 'You're making a dog's breakfast of the working, causing vast amounts of delay to people who've paid a small fortune to travel on our best train. You obviously need someone to teach you your business. You don't know signalling regulations and you're trying to send men over a route for which they have no route knowledge.'

'Do you know who you are talking to?' he asked in his haughtiest voice. 'I am the Chief Controller.'

'In which case you ought to know better! Have you thought how long it will take to get a Pilot driver down to Castle Cary to take that Old Oak man down to Yeovil Junction? Have you thought of the difficulties you'll create at Exeter St David's when that train arrives from the Southern — facing the wrong way for Penzance?'

'I shall not be spoken to like this,' he blustered, 'give me your name — I shall report you for foul language.'

I told him my name — though I had no idea who he was — and put the phone down. Five minutes later the Cornish Riviera continued on its journey via Somerton. In my diary for 6 August I wrote: 'The weather is getting hotter and the railway seems to be getting even madder. I wonder if this is leading to a climax?' That was the day that 'Sunshine' came into Witham box and in the course of a telephone conversation with a Supervisor at Westbury — the train service was in chaos — called him by the choicest variety of names, most of them obscene. At 11 a.m. on the 7th the thermometer in Witham box registered 90 degrees Fahrenheit. According to an extract from the Shops & Offices Act pinned up close by it was illegal to work in a room at that temperature. We frequently joked about this silly rule — as if we could all walk out and go home, the very idea! The train service that day included four excursions, three of them for Weymouth. The entire down-line service was out of gear resulting from a brake failure on the 7.30 a.m. Paddington at Westbury, a hot axle-box on the 7.51 a.m. Paddington excursion and a false fire alarm on the 7.51 a.m. Bristol to Weymouth DMU. The weather was hot enough to have triggered it. First Yeovil and then Castle Cary suffered points failures. The junction points at Castle Cary lay for the Weymouth line and the operating lever was locked in position by a track-circuit failure. The young signalman there was so scared of 'Sunshine' that he would not break the glass on the sealed 'release' plunger without the great man's permission and so the West of England main line suffered further delay until the man could be contacted and asked to telephone his blessing to the trembling signalman at Castle Cary. Bullying stifles initiative.

By 2 p.m. the temperature in Witham box was 96 degrees Fahrenheit and the rail temperature, measured by the Permanent-Way Department patrolman, was 120 degrees Fahrenheit. The long-welded rails had expanded so much that their expansion joints were closed tight. At Departmental discretion a speed restriction could have been placed on those sections of track which were so badly affected by the weather but this was not considered necessary. A man was continuously patrolling each of the lengths concerned. At 5.10 p.m. the 3.30 p.m. Paddington express stopped at Witham and the driver shouted this message to me: 'About half a mile from Blatchbridge down home but in the up main, there is a buckle in the track.' This is precisely what was said. It sounded odd so, very hot and bothered near the end of a long shift, I ran down the stairs, climbed onto the engine and asked him to repeat. Slowly and patiently, as if speaking to a child, he did so, word for word. There was something wrong — I knew — yet I could not see what it was so I asked him yet again and he repeated the message exactly. Feeling that I was being very stupid I decided what I thought he was saying and let him go. Back in the box I told Chris Burden at Blatchbridge to send me 'Obstruction Danger' and told him that, half a mile on the approach side of his up home signal the track was buckled.

Chris had a 'light' engine on the downline, waiting for the 3.30 Paddington to clear so he informed its driver what had occurred and asked him to go through cautiously and examine the up line for any defects. In the meantime the 12.35 p.m. Penzance came to a stand at Witham, outside the box. The driver of the 'light' engine arrived and its driver reported to me that he had seen nothing at all wrong with the up line. I explained what had happened to the driver of the up 'fast' and sent him on his way. Half a mile *after* passing Blatchbridge up home signal the Penzance went over the buckled track. Luckily, both rails of the up main had slewed the same way under the intense compression forces at work in the over-heated steel so that they were still 'to gauge' but displaced about four inches towards the down line. The driver of the Penzance stopped and reported matters to the signalman at Clink Road.

I was shocked when I was told and realised then what was missing from that message. The driver had not said on which side of the signal the buckled track lay and because he had stopped at my box I assumed it lay between Blatchbridge and me. He obviously thought he could not stop smoothly in the half-mile between track defect and Blatchbridge box and he was wrong in not explaining matters better, especially when he saw I was puzzled. But I was wrong in trying to place a rational explanation on what I knew was a garbled message. Normally, when long-welded track buckles, the rails 'explode' left and right from their fastenings. I and a train-load of people had

been very lucky. The driver of the 'light' engine must have been
blind not to have seen the bulge in the track as he came slowly
down to Blatchbridge home signal but his eyesight was not my
concern. I had dropped a great big clanger and I hated myself
for so doing.

The Permanent-Way Department cut lengths out of the rails
in order to be able to slew it straight but at first the gaps they
created closed up such were the forces within the rail. In the
meantime all up trains were diverted via Frome. At 8.42 p.m.
the track was temporarily repaired and trains were allowed to
run normally — as far as the Permanent-Way Department was
concerned — but Tom Baber was on duty at Blatchbridge by
then and he was having none of it. Each up train was stopped
and its driver warned to go over the track cautiously. The
Chief Controller rang Tom to remonstrate with him. Tom
replied, 'You might be the Chief Controller, Mister, an' I dun't
care whether you be or you b'aint, you can't order me to do
what aint safe. That track has only been put back straight, it
hasn't been re-stressed so it could buckle again, it's hot enough
for it. As long as I'm on duty they'll go over that at 20 mph till
the "P-Way" have done a proper job.'

A few days later I was served with a summons to go to
Bristol to answer the laughable charge of 'swearing at the
Chief Controller' and the decidedly un-funny charge of 'failing
to advise Blatchbridge Junction signalman of defective track'.
This was the very rock bottom for me. I had been having a
signalman's nightmare thinking about what might have hap-
pened to that train but for the merest fluke of good fortune and
I decided that the time had come to leave the railway.

The hearing was appointed for 1 September at 9 a.m.
Unfortunately I had planned to go to Toddington that morning to photograph the preserved steam engines *Princess Elizabeth* and *Clan Line* on their way back from the Darlington
'Rail 150' celebrations and I had no intention of missing this
just to go to Bristol for a session with 'Sunshine'. I told him I
was taking Susan to hospital that morning and asked for the
hearing to be put back to two o'clock. It was. I went to

Toddington, the engines ran four hours late and I only just got to Bristol in time for the hearing. The 'court' consisted of 'Sunshine' and his Boss. First they dealt with the matter of swearing at the Chief Controller. 'What have you to say about that?'

'Of course I swore at him. So would you have done if you'd been in Witham box.'

'Are you suggesting that we would use foul language?' asked the Boss man primly.

'Your colleague sitting next to you is a past master. You should've heard him in my box a couple of weeks ago.' I could not hide a certain levity in my voice.

'Mr Vaughan!' snapped the Boss man. 'This is a place of discipline and correction.'

His hypocrisy quite took my breath away. He knew perfectly well that the railway ran on tea and 'foul language'. 'Sunshine' weighed in as I gasped. 'The Chief Controller was perfectly correct in wanting to divert that train. There was vandalism on the line ahead.'

'There is nothing in regulations requiring special precautions over vandalism. The word does not even occur. Regulation fifteen took care of that situation and if you want us to make special precautions you'll have to write us the rule. We can't obey a rule that doesn't exist.'

Boss man cut in. 'Yes, all right, he's admitted he swore at the Chief Controller. Now, what about the matter of the buckled track?'

I admitted at once that I had made a serious error in so far as I placed a meaning on a garbled message so as to make it make sense.

Two heads swivelled inwards as if driven by one motor. 'Well — he's admitted it,' said the Boss man. They seemed surprised or disappointed or both. They were whispering together. Perhaps they expected me to make excuses, blame others, wriggle out of it. Maybe that is what they would have done. But what did they know of me? What did they know about weeks of twelve-hour shifts in sweltering conditions trying to run a shambles of a railway they were supposed to be managing? I had never seen the Boss man before and I had never had a conversation with 'Sunshine'. These pontiffs sitting in judgement made me furious. They knew damn-all as far as I was concerned. The Boss man's voice cut through my indignant thoughts.

'Will you take a reprimand?' He spoke as if he was offering me a slice of cake. I was bitterly disappointed with myself, that my railway service should have to end with a black mark, my head was full of this and I do not recall what I replied. 'Please yourself,' in all probability. When I got home I wrote my resignation for a month ahead and posted it to the Office at Westbury.

During September the weather became cooler. The days slipped away like the leaves that blew down off the roadside trees and at ten o'clock on 4 October 1975 I said good-bye to my mate and walked down the steps of Witham signal box for the last time.

APPENDIX 1

Equipment failures at Challow signal box
29/4/64 to 10/6/64

12/5/64 Points 20 failed to return to 'Normal' 1.20 p.m. In order 2.10 p.m. Caused by broken bolt head securing 'chair' to sleeper.

16/5/64 Wire broke whilst lever 8 was being pulled at 4.29. In order 7.30 p.m.

30/5/64 Track circuit failed locking signals 2 and 7. 11.22 a.m. In order 12.30 p.m.

3/6/64 Light out in No 54 signal at 6 a.m. Lamp filled and re-lit.

6/6/64 Wire broke whilst lever 5 was being pulled at 8.52 a.m. In order 10.52 a.m.

10/6/64 Signal 59 failed to respond to lever at 11.50 a.m. In order 12.35 p.m.

APPENDIX 2

Weight of metals comprising 6807 *Birchwood Grange* and tender

	6807			Tender		
	Tons	*cwt*	*qr*	*Tons*	*cwt*	*qr*
Steel	57	13	2	16	6	2
Cast iron	5	10	0	1	16	0
Gun metal	1	2	1	—	—	—
Brass	0	0	3	—	—	—
White metal	0	1	3	0	0	1
Bronze	0	5	0	0	1	2
Copper	2	9	2	0	0	3
Hardened lead	1	10	1	—	—	—
	68	13	0	18	5	0

qr = quarter or 28lb

APPENDIX 3

Freight Train Derailments
(Condensed from Report E.572D *A Statistical Analysis of Freight Train Derailments*, British Railways, June 1966)

The first indication that anything was seriously wrong with the vehicle fleet was given by the large number of BR 211 Pallet van derailments before 1961. These were regarded as a special case rather than an indication of a more widespread trend for the future and now a reality. These have increased because of the increase in speed since dieselisation has imposed a duty which is appreciably more arduous for the present wagon fleet. The majority of designs with a high derailment rate have eyebolt suspension, this type of suspension combined with high speed produces derailments. The BR 211 Pallet van with eyebolt suspension has produced more plain track derailments since 1958 than the BR 108 (16-ton) coal wagon although there are over 100 times more coal wagons than Pallet vans. The BR 240 Banana van eyebolt suspension caused six derailments 1958–64 when only 200 such vehicles were in existence. They have since been scrapped and the BR 211 fleet has been withdrawn pending modification of their suspension. Between 1958 and 1962, both years inclusive, 40,965 vacuum braked, 10 ft wheelbase wagons with eyebolt suspension have caused 49 derailments and of these 20 were caused by BR 211 Pallet van although only 1935 of these existed. In the same period 106,115 vacuum-braked wagons with 10ft wheelbase and shoe suspension caused 30 derailments. Poorly designed suspension being adversely effected by relatively high speed was but one factor, a list of causes and the number of derailments attributed annually to those causes is given opposite.

Causes of all plain track derailments of short wheelbase vehicles (i.e. 10ft or less)

Cause	1963	1964	1965
Broken or defective springs	4	6	15
Broken axle	0	0	1
Hot axle box	0	4	2
Other axle-box defect	2	1	3
Any other defect	1	3	5
Track only	4	3	13
Excess speed only	2	0	3
Driver error other than excess speed	2	4	14
Driver error including excess speed	1	0	0
Speed and track defect	5	3	2
Speed and vehicle defect	1	2	1
Vehicle and track defect	7	10	6
Faulty loading	3	0	5
Undetermined including derailments with 3 or more causes given	6	8	10
	38	44	80

Plain track derailments steam/diesel hauled 1963

Traction	Derails	Millions of steam freight train miles	No. of derails per million train miles
Steam	14	71.714	0.20
Diesel	22	31.879	0.69

If there were no real difference between the derailment proneness of the steam and diesel hauled trains the expected distribution of the 36 derailments would be: Steam 25, Diesel 11

1964

Steam	9	54.662	0.16
Diesel	34	43.468	0.78

Expected distribution of the 43 derailments: Steam 24, Diesel 19

1965

Steam	7	33.437	0.21
Diesel	69	52.996	1.3

Expected distribution of the 76 derailments: Steam 29, Diesel 47

APPENDIX 4

Trains passing Witham 14.00–22.00hrs, 9 May 1975
(A. Vaughan on duty)

TRAIN	BELL CODE	TIME	ENGINE	REMARKS
1B55 12.30 Paddington	4	14.14	1046	Right time
Westbury–Merehead	5–1–3	14.40	1023	To branch
1A19 11.00 Penzance	4	14.55	1009	3 minutes early
1B65 13.30 Paddington	4	15.01	1056	5 minutes early
60— 12.30 Exeter	5	15.14	47160	To Up Siding. Pick up 16 tanks
Westbury–Merehead	5–1–3	15.28	1069	To branch ex-Loop at 15.39
1A25 11.15 Penzance (FO)	4	15.32	1071	5 minutes early. Belled on 4–1–3
60— 12.30 Exeter	—	15.37	47160	ex-Up Siding. 26 = 635 tons
Merehead–Botley	—	16.00	1033	ex-Branch to Up Main 16.05
1A29 13.55 Paignton	4	16.02	1015	9 minutes late. Belled on 4–1–3
1B73 14.30 Paddington	4	16.17	1051	Right time
Merehead–Brentford	—	17.07	1069	ex-Branch to Up Main 17.17. 3–2
7B28 Bristol–Yeovil	3–2–1–2	17.07	Cl.25	180 minutes late
2060 16.03 Bristol	3–1–1–2	17.27	Cl.31	5 minutes late. To Weymouth
Westbury–Merehead	5–1–3	17.36	1029	To Branch
Westbury–Merehead	5–1–3	17.43	47001	To Up Siding. Stable empty wagons
1A45 12.35 Penzance	4	17.47	47086	50 minutes late
2v66 16.20 Weymouth	3–1–1–2	18.03	DMU	15 minutes late 3–1–1–2
1A65 15.55 Paignton	4	18.12	50019	14 minutes late
Light engine to Wx	—	18.16	47001	ex-Up Siding. Belled on 2–3
1B93 16.30 Paddington	4	18.18	1053	4 minutes late
Merehead–Acton	—	18.38	Cl.52	ex-Branch to Up Main 18.47 5
Westbury–Merehead	5–1–3	18.38	Cl.47	ex-Loop to Branch 18.49
1B05 16.53 Paddington (FO)	4	18.45	1041	4 minutes late
1B19 17.30 Paddington	4	19.00	50049	Right time. The 'Golden Hind'
2061 17.45 Bristol	3–1–1–2	19.18	DMU	3 minutes late. To Weymouth
1A79 14.40 Penzance	4	19.20/47	50028	23/50 late. 50028 to Up Siding

19.20 Wx–Merehead	5–1–3	19.25	47061	To Up Siding. 47061 to 1A79
19.07 Wx–Yeovil	5–1–2	19.42	1005	
2v70 17.45 Weymouth	3–1–1–2	19.55	DMU	25 minutes late. 3–1–1–2
Merehead–Theale	—	19.55	—	To Up Siding. Engine to 50028
'1 live, 1 dead' to Wx	—	20.00	Engine	ex-'Theale' and 50028
1B39 18.27 Paddington (FO)	4	20.05	1005	Right time. To Truro
6075 19.25 Tiverton Junction	5	20.11	Cl.33	55 minutes early
Light engine to Merehead	2–3–1–3	20.23	47078	To Up Siding for 19.20 Wx.
1B43 18.30 Paddington	4	20.30	—	10 minutes late
1A09 16.10 Penzance	4	20.45	1026	3 minutes late
2v72 19.40 Weymouth	3–1–1–2	21.25	Cl.31	Right time. Belled on 3–1–1–2
Merehead–Wootton Bassett	—	21.25	Cl.47	ex-Loop to Up Main 21.31. 5 bells
1B55 19.30 Paddington	4	21.33	Cl.50	13 minutes late
4A13 14.45 Penzance	3–1–1	21.41	—	Right time. Perishables to Paddington
2062 20.08 Bristol	3–1–1–2	21.50	DMU	20 minutes late. Belled 3–1–1–2

A fairly busy shift. I was able to deal very promptly with the failure of 50028 on the 14.40 Penzance and had some extra shunting to do as a result of 'borrowing' the engine off the 19.20 Westbury. Some rapid clearances of down trains to the down loop when passenger trains were running close behind and a successful afternoon of feeding up goods trains from branch to up main without delaying following passenger trains. A lot of bells, a lot of lever pulling – a lot of conversation on the telephone to make arrangements continuously. A typically successful shift 'playing trains'. There were several thousand more shifts like this in my fifteen years as a signalman. Sometimes things went wrong. That's life.

Names of the Locomotives given above

1005	*Western Venturer*	1046	*Western Marquis*
1009	*Western Invader*	1053	*Western Patriarch*
1015	*Western Champion*	1056	*Western Sultan*
1023	*Western Fusilier*	1058	*Western Nobleman*
1026	*Western Centurion*	1069	*Western Vanguard*
1029	*Western Legionnaire*	1071	*Western Renown*
1033	*Western Trooper*	47078	*George Jackson Churchward*
1041	*Western Prince*	47086	*Colossus*

INDEX